Ruth V. Hemenway, M.D.

Ruth V. Hemenway, M.D.

A Memoir of Revolutionary China, 1924–1941

Edited with an introduction by Fred W. Drake

The University of Massachusetts Press   Amherst, 1977

Library of Congress Catalog Card Number 76-45245
ISBN 0-87023-230-4
Printed in the United States of America
Designed by Mary Mendell
Library of Congress Cataloging in Publication Data
appear on the last printed page of this book.

Acknowledgments

Acknowledgment is made to the following, with deep appreciation for their assistance:
Mirium Albertson, M.D.; Mr. and Mrs. Len Allen; Mr. and Mrs. Brewster Bingham; Mr. and Mrs. Lewis Black; Miss Julie Brodhead; Rachel Chin; Mr. and Mrs. James Halberstadt; Dorthea Hayden; Mrs. Carl Hemenway; Mrs. Rene Hemmes; Mrs. Louis Horst; Leila Hyde; Mr. and Mrs. Larue H. Kemper; Mr. and Mrs. Chester Kmit; Irene Koeneke; Mrs. D. MacDonald-Millar; Claire and Ed Manwell; Catherine Merritt; Mr. and Mrs. Merrill Mundell, Sr.; Mr. and Mrs. Merrill A. Mundell; Gen. and Mrs. Lunsford Oliver; Charlotte Otis; Jacob Rietsema; Mrs. Lois Scott; Mrs. Leon Shumway; Miss Lucy Ann Taylor; Mrs. Leon Tiley; Mrs. Tufts; Mrs. Jean York; The Grace Harris Memorial; The Williamsburg Brush and Palette Club.

Contents

Illustrations

Introduction

Dr. Ruth V. Hemenway's graphic account of her life in China as a physician, surgeon, teacher, and observer during eighteen critical years before the Communist revolution (1924–1941) is a remarkable document. It is rich with poignant and perceptive pictures of Chinese village life in the southeastern province of Fukien, of modernized urban life in the Kuomintang-controlled Yangtze Valley on the eve of the Japanese invasion in 1937, and of the besieged wartime capital of Chungking in western China. In all of these settings, sometimes witnessing horrible scenes born of poverty and ignorance or even of bandit brutality, Dr. Hemenway perceived the positive aspects of Chinese life, including the quiet strength and great potential of the Chinese people.

While her book presents a fascinating panorama of Chinese conditions, it is also a frank testimony to the strengths and weaknesses of the Western missionary enterprise in China, which Dr. Hemenway joined even though she was skeptical of the goal to convert China. Her dream was to aid a people in need. She hoped that by introducing modern medicine and rudimentary science to rural areas, she would alleviate some of the suffering that accompanied the political turmoil, economic chaos, and social breakdown that characterized China in the early decades of the twentieth century. During her years of medical work in the villages of Fukien, Ruth Hemenway grew increasingly alienated from the goals and practices of organized Christianity. Yet she continued her work with the firm belief that, with or without the aid of Christian missionaries, the combination of modern knowledge and ancient Chinese traditions would produce a new China of hope, vigor, and success.

Ruth V. Hemenway (1894–1974) was raised on her father's 100-acre farm in the village of Williamsburg, Massachusetts. In contrast to her hard-working father, who rarely left his farm in the Berkshire hills, she was drawn to a larger world. Her teacher-mother had introduced her to books as a young child, and Ruth proved to be uncommonly and persistently inquisitive. Before she was thirteen she had acquired a deep sense of alienation from the religious fundamentalism of New England village life. After graduating from Northampton High School in 1910, she taught in the one-room schoolhouse in Conway and later in the Williamsburg-Searsville School in order to save enough money to pursue her childhood dream of studying medicine in Boston.

Endowed with a New Englander's capacity for hard work, Ruth earned her way at Tufts Medical School by waiting on tables in a small private girls' school in Back Bay. While her intellectual life was imbued with Western rationalism, she thirsted for a religious truth beyond the confines of Christian fundamentalism. Scornful of comfort, she rejected America's coming age of ease, and sought to pursue her religious quest through service to mankind. Before she graduated in 1921, Ruth had decided that China's medical needs were greater than those of her homeland, and she resolved to practice medicine in the Middle Kingdom.

The question was how to get to China. After interning at the Women's Medical College in Philadelphia and at the Pennsylvania State Hospital in Allentown, she at last found her opportunity. Though she felt an antipathy toward organized religion, Ruth needed organizational

backing for her work in China. Thus, in 1924 she accepted support from The Grace Harris Memorial and an appointment from the Methodist Women's Board of Foreign Missions to direct a 100-bed hospital for women in Mintsing, Fukien.

She entered the coastal province of Fukien, opposite Taiwan, in an era of crisis. The ancient Chinese empire that had collapsed with the Manchu Ch'ing dynasty just twelve years before was not easily replaced. Political parties, warlords, and bandits battled one another for local control. The result was turmoil and hardship for the Chinese masses who yearned for the return of order and for modern improvements.

When she arrived in warlord-dominated China in 1924, Ruth Hemenway was innocent regarding the nature of Chinese politics. Yet, though she lacked a comprehensive view of the emerging struggle for

Chinese reunification, as a keen observer of the local scene in Fukien she realized that great changes were imminent. She felt the local repercussions when Sun Yat-sen's Nationalist party (Kuomintang), temporarily in league with the then small Chinese Communist party, launched the "Northern Expedition" from its Canton base in 1926 in an attempt to restore a central government to divided China. Armies crisscrossed Fukien, while warlord troops metamorphosed into Nationalists; bandit and communist forces were seemingly indistinguishable; missionaries became convenient targets of the campaign's antiforeignism; confusion abounded.

When a quasi-unification of China was achieved in 1928 by the new Nanking government of Chiang Kai-shek, Ruth hoped that this new order would promote the modernization and progress that China so desperately needed. She was aware of the superficiality of the Nationalist government's programs, which sought modernization of the cities before systematically addressing the problems of the countryside. But contrasted with the despair and lack of progress she had witnessed during the warlord period, these programs gave her hope that China's regeneration was finally under way. The new government was striving to consolidate its position and to effect a real Chinese unity. It was negotiating new treaties that gradually reduced the privileges wrested from a weak China by foreign powers during the nineteenth and early twentieth centuries. By 1933 the government had fully regained tariff autonomy and had ended foreign control of the Maritime Customs and the Salt Revenue Administration.

More significantly to Ruth Hemenway, the Nationalist government appeared to be attracting and supporting China's most dedicated reform-minded leaders. Even Westerners and their knowledge were given an important place by the new regime. Ruth was enthusiastic over the New Life movement, launched in 1934, which sought China's regeneration through the resuscitation of ancient Confucian virtues and the use of a variety of Y.M.C.A. methods. She did not know that much of the movement's inspiration was based on the negative aim of competing with the reform ideology of the communists, whom Chiang had expelled from his party in 1927.

Yet she identified with and remained deeply concerned over the plight of China's peasantry. On her arrival in China she had not remained in the relative safety and comfort of the treaty ports, whose attractions appealed to many missionaries. Instead she had worked for the first decade of her career in the remote hill villages of the upper Min Valley, 75 miles inland from Foochow. There she observed not only the obvious failures of traditional village life, but also the potential of such rural communities—in which 80 percent of China's population lived—for a rebirth that ultimately supported China's modern revolution and emergence as a modern state. Using her church affiliation as an organizational means to help the peasantry in their time of need, Ruth realized, unlike many of her missionary colleagues, that the common people of China possessed strengths that were not dependent on the Christian message. She believed in their ability to improve their lives with new organization and modern knowledge.

She was not a political revolutionary; yet her work in establishing village health facilities and paramedical teams in Fukien, as well as her programs to educate villagers in elementary hygiene and science, anticipated many of the activities that have been supported by the People's Republic of China. She recognized, as did few other Westerners at the time, that China's salvation must have a rural focus and that it must be based on the common people. In this belief she was in agreement with the young Mao Tse-tung (though she had not heard of him at the time and considered the communists to be little more than bandits), who was then organizing a peasant-based revolution in Kiangsi, just west of Mintsing.

When she left Shanghai in 1941, after China had already suffered four tragic years of war with Japan, Ruth Hemenway did not know that she would never return to the rugged hills of Fukien or to the awe-inspiring Yangtze gorges through which she had traveled during the war. But China would not let her go; it remained a part of her. It educated her to the truth of the universality of human worth regardless of race or religion, and caused her to remain, for the rest of her life, a firm believer in the unconquerable spirit of mankind.

Although Ruth kept occupied with her medical work in Williamsburg and Northampton, she was haunted by scenes from her past life. As if to exorcise these memories, she began to study watercolor painting in the 1950s with Stephen L. Hamilton of Amherst. Blessed with a natural sense of composition, she produced paintings of her life in China that received acclaim both locally and in Boston for their vividness and evocative qualities. (Stephen Hamilton and I have selected a few of these unusual visual records to illustrate this memoir.) Like her memoirs to which they refer, these paintings portray the contrasts that characterized China at the time: the everyday activities of peace-loving peasants contrasted with the horrors of bandit attacks; the serene beauty of the Yangtze with the hard labor of the trackers; the joy of children flying kites with the hopelessness of prisoners in the village jail of Mintsing; the shrubs, camphor tree, and placid white walls of the hospital compound in Mintsing with the grim colors and stark angles dramatizing the shriek of destruction and death after a bombing in Chungking.

I was privileged to become acquainted with Dr. Hemenway shortly before her death. Once when I asked to hear more details of her life in China, with a twinkle in her eye she produced a massive manuscript she had written in the 1950s, based on her China diaries (now held in The Sophia Smith Collection, Smith College). I found it a compelling document, not only for the immediacy and accuracy of its description of Chinese rural life in a time of upheaval, but also for its unusual reflections on the missionary endeavor. I suggested that she make her story available to the public; she agreed and asked me for editorial help. Unfortunately, her life ended before this work was finished. Thus without her collaboration I reduced the original manuscript by about two-thirds, and added footnotes. In the considerable editorial work that resulted, however, I have attempted throughout to preserve the intent and flavor of the original. My work was made less difficult due to the kind assistance of Dr. Hemenway's family and friends, particularly Mr. and Mrs. Neng-wong Chin, Mr. Stephen Hamilton, and Mrs. Sally Mundell.

Blessed with a rational and inquiring mind that appreciated the humor of her situation even in the midst of pain and horror, Ruth V. Hemenway has given us a salient record of a remarkable American woman in China during a period of prodigious change.

FRED W. DRAKE
Amherst, Massachusetts
September 1976

I

From New England to China

I STOOD ALONE on the Shanghai wharf at midnight in January 1924. The bitter cold permeated my bones and the inky darkness wrapped itself around me as I gazed apprehensively at the dimly lighted Chinese boat looming above me and listened to the strange and mysterious crew chattering in an alien language. I was a medical missionary on my way to the interior of Fukien Province, to a new and unknown country far from the familiar things that had made up my world. Now the boat that was to carry me to my new life lay ready while I shivered with cold and panic, unable to start my feet up the gangplank.

Suddenly two Chinese girls came tripping down to the wharf. Dr. Yen-yü Huang, with whom I had interned in Philadelphia, and her nurse friend, Anna Tsai, had come to see me off. The sight of their smiling faces and their arms filled with farewell gifts dispelled my fears. With happy laughter and words of advice for the trip, they gave me moral courage to climb the gangplank and to take the last irretrievable steps toward my life as a missionary. As the boat pulled slowly away from shore they called to me through the darkness, "You do not go alone. God goes with you."

I felt shame for my weakness. These two, whose childhoods had been untouched by missionary zeal, had become Christians during their years of medical training; now they sent a strong challenge across the widening dark water to the Yankee girl with centuries of Christian background. They did not know that, despite this inheritance and teaching, I was not sure what God was. For my mind seethed with questions even as I found comfort and security in the traditional God of heaven. Indeed, it was this questioning, this seeking for truth, which was indirectly responsible for my going to China. Surely in Christian service I would find the answers.

The lumbering boat wallowed southward for two days and nights. No one spoke English and I knew not a word of Chinese. All the first day I lay in a steamer chair on deck, warmed by the sun, wondering about missionary life. I remembered the day when I was about eleven that I was cleaning an antique desk with an intriguing little cupboard at its base. Unlocking the small door, I discovered an old Tufts Medical School bulletin and sat down on the floor to study it from cover to cover. When I finished I knew that medicine was to be my life work.

My father was a hard-working New England farmer who happily cultivated his hundred acres of stony hillside in Williamsburg, Massachusetts, where he provided a comfortable living for his family of seven. He was a very silent man, most undemonstrative, busy all day long and hidden behind a newspaper at night. I do not recall ever having a conversation with him, but always I followed him around in his fields or rode to market with him. I used to look at him with his jet black hair, his shining black eyes and very white skin, wondering what he thought about things. But I never knew.

Mother had blue eyes and brown hair, loved to read, and attended church every Sunday with her five children, in spite of my father's angry protests. There were many quarrels over this subject, but we children never knew why church attendance was a matter of urgency for one parent and the subject of real opposition by the other. Dreams and aspirations were not subjects for conversation; religion and sex were never discussed. I learned very early in life to keep my deep thoughts to myself.

I finished high school and silently followed my goal toward medical school. This meant teaching school for three years to save enough for the first year's tuition in the premedical course. German would be needed in order to enter, so in the evenings after school I drove three miles with horse and buggy to Williamsburg center where I took a trolley car eight miles to Northampton for the course at People's Institute.

When the great day of my acceptance to medical school came, I told my parents I was going to Boston to study medicine and waited for their objections. None came. They were simply bewildered that a girl should want to study medicine. But if that was what I wanted, and if I had saved the money for it, they had no objections.

That fall I walked proudly through the corridors of Tufts Medical School and paid down the first year's tuition. That I had only ten dollars left to face the coming year did not disturb me. It was easy to find work in Boston and soon I was waiting on tables to pay for my food and room. I pursued my studies completely fascinated with this new life of study, work, and congenial classmates. It was not an easy life, but it was a very happy one.

One Sunday during my junior year in 1920 I took a walk to rest my mind and eyes before plunging into an evening of study. Strolling down Tremont Street to Columbus Avenue, I noticed a gray-stone church with a big placard by the door announcing that Dr. Mary Stone,* a Chinese woman medical doctor, was to speak at that very hour. Full of curiosity, I entered the church and found a seat in the gallery.

* Mary Stone [Shih Mei-yü, 1873–1954], daughter of early Protestant converts in central China, began her medical training in the United States in 1892 at the University of Michigan. In 1896 she and Ida Kahn [K'ang Ch'eng] became the first Chinese women to obtain American medical degrees. Both served as pioneer women doctors in China.

Dr. Hemenway, Tufts Medical School graduate, 1921 (above), and at age 10 (below).

Dr. Hemenway and child, 1924 (above), and with Mintsing Hospital staff (below). Cung Dai pictured on far left.

For the next hour I listened to that tiny courageous woman telling of her country's needs, of the millions who suffered needlessly and hopelessly for lack of medical care, of thousands of infants who died at birth and young mothers infected at birth by ignorant midwives. Hordes of the blind, doomed to a life of beggary and hunger, marched before my eyes as she talked. I could hear the screams of the insane, locked in dark rooms or chained to posts or even killed by their families who did not know how to treat them. I learned of whole villages wiped out by pestilence, and whole provinces decimated by flood and famine. Before Dr. Stone was through talking I knew I would give my strength and knowledge to medical work in China.

I graduated from Tufts Medical School in 1921. I had only fifty cents left—not enough for train fare to Williamsburg! It never occurred to me to borrow from anyone. I carried my suitcase from Roxbury down Huntington Avenue to the Public Library where I studied a newspaper and found myself a job at Franklin Square House for women.

When I went to Philadelphia for my internship I learned that Dr. Mary Stone had also been an inspirational figure for one of my Chinese colleagues. This intern was a beautiful young girl, Dr. Yen-yü Huang. When she asked me of my plans for the future, I told her of Dr. Stone and my decision. To my surprise she answered that Dr. Stone had influenced her, too, to study medicine and to come to the United States for further study.

"Conditions in China are tragic," she said softly. "China needs doctors and nurses to teach and to heal. Yours is a noble decision. However, you must be very sure that this is what you want to do. It is not an easy life."

"I know this is my future," I told her. "I am sure it is not easy, but what is worthwhile is rarely easy."

Dr. Huang gave me the address of a mission society in New York City to which I might apply to be sent to China. I made out the application and furnished references. Three weeks later a brief, curt note arrived stating that the society took only Methodists for the mission field.

My application had stated that I was Congregationalist, although I had never felt very clear about the tenets of the church. In fact many of them seemed illogical and irrelevant. Why should the fact, if fact it were, of a man born of a virgin and returning to earth after his death provide any basis for a religion? Perhaps he was so born; perhaps he did return to earth. What did that have to do with religion? The foundation for a religion must be one's philosophy toward life, one's deepest attitudes towards people and events. How could myth or miracle build that base? But I never expressed these thoughts to anyone, thinking that people would consider them heretical.

Faced with this ridiculous situation—being refused because I was a Congregationalist rather than a Methodist—I decided it was easier to become a Methodist than to make out a new application and seek a dozen new references. This done, the Board of Directors of the Methodist Mission summoned me to New York for a conference.

Someone ushered me into a large room where a formidable group of perhaps a dozen women dressed in black sat around a long table. After some moments of silent scrutiny they asked me to be seated. There were routine questions—my age, health, and medical training. Then came the question, "Have you had any Bible study?" I hesitated. Mother had grounded her five children thoroughly in the Bible. But I had a feeling the good women would not consider that of any value. I told them I never had had any courses in Bible. The women in black consulted together with troubled faces.

As I awaited their decision my thoughts drifted back to the dreadful Sunday school sessions of my childhood, to the teacher's dogmatic assertions which my questioning mind refused to accept as logical. How could there be truth without logic? I sat silent and sullen the long boring hour every Sunday. Then I was thirteen. One day the teacher commented on a battle in the Old Testament and announced that this tale proved whichever army believed in God would win. All my repressed rebellion and resentment came boiling over, and I asked angrily, "What if both armies believed in God?" Teacher eyed me sternly and made no reply. A fearful silence settled over the class. Somehow I got out of the room, never to go back, feeling as alienated as a leper.

The women in black had finished their consultation. I looked around the room at their stern faces. I wondered whether a doctor would prove unacceptable if she had not had a Bible course. They asked me whether I would be willing to take a correspondence course in Bible and I replied positively. I thought to myself that not only would I be willing to take it if it was necessary, but also I would be deeply interested in discovering the nature of such a course. There followed another short, whispered consultation. And then I was in!

My family took the news of my imminent departure for China as phlegmatically as they had accepted the idea of my studying medicine. They were not interested in my reasons, only in the fact of my going. We were New Englanders who never showed our emotions—except anger—and never talked about inner thoughts. How could we understand each other?

My sister Rachel and I had often joked about missionaries, those people who were paid less than janitors or cleaning women, and who gave up a good life in the United States to go to outlandish places to win the "heathen" from *his* religion and convince him that *ours* was the only true one. Now I was one of those people. I silently vowed that I would try to understand those to whom I went to teach a healthier way of life, but never, never would I push them into believing what I was supposed to believe. In fact I did not know what I believed, only what I questioned. I had only negative and rebellious thoughts, nothing to share with anyone.

Now I was lying in the steamer chair on the deck of the old steamer, lumbering southward toward Fukien Province just west of Formosa. I thought that even though we could not talk with each other, I was going to do something for this strange assortment of fellow passengers. I brought out my portable victrola and played records for them. The steerage passengers crowded to the dividing fence while servants stood in the doorways and our privileged passengers lolled in their easy chairs. They all listened with great solemnity to my classical records. Then I switched to popular music and their faces glowed with pleasure as I played such gems as "Three O'Clock in the Morning" and "Yes, We Have No Bananas Today." Encouraged by their reactions, I changed to hymns. One by one my audience disappeared.

At the end of the second day, when the setting sun was purpling the barren, brown hills on the little island to our left, the shoreline emerged on our right, and presently we entered the mouth of the Min River. A junk laden with logs floated into sight—an unwieldy craft with three square, white sails and with its hull bright in red and blue paint. Still more logs were roped together in great bundles on each side of the ship and hung just low enough to float on the surface of the water. Beyond the junk were small boats with red, gray, or brown sails, sitting motionless on the smooth, yellow water hemmed in by high mountains.

We cast anchor. Small boats swooped down on us like gay butterflies around a flower. Some of them were manned by barefooted women, while bright little children sat quietly on the decks with ropes around their waists to pull them up if they fell overboard. Their sparkling black eyes watched everything going on around them. I stood alone on the upper deck watching the scrambling passengers getting themselves and their baggage transferred from our boat to the colorful small craft around us.

After an hour of this, a houseboat with sails moved up to our vessel and two Caucasian women in old-fashioned clothes waved to me. As I waved back I had a vision of myself five years hence returning to the States in the clothes I was now wearing.

"Are you Ruth Hemenway?" one of them called up to me.

"Yes, have you come to rescue me?" I shouted down to her.

"We are nurses from Magaw Hospital in Foochow, and we volunteered to meet the new missionary," they explained as their messenger-boy scrambled onto my boat. It was a wonderful experience to sit in the tiny cabin of their houseboat and to chatter about the States, as well as about their work in Foochow. Finally it was late afternoon, and I asked when our boat would start upriver for the city.

"We have to wait for the tide," they explained. "It is only ten miles but it takes time. We left there last night to meet you this afternoon, and it will be one o'clock tomorrow morning before the tide will be right for the return trip."

They showed me their great bamboo baskets packed with bedding and food for this twenty-mile expedition. It was the revelation of a speed to which I was not geared. I pondered, wondering how my quick and efficient way of doing things could be slowed to the oriental tempo. In spite of the terrific medical need, I must learn to travel in first gear and not fret over it. It would take some doing.

We had a pleasant meal of sandwiches made the night before, cake, and tea. Then I played my records to them until they proposed sleep. Years later one of the nurses, Frieda Staubli, told me they were furious with my record playing because they were so hungry for news from the States, and I was too unperceptive to see it. At four in the morning I awoke to find our boat already anchored at shore in the midst of the city. Excitedly I awoke the girls in the other bunks and the boatmen who remained deeply asleep on the deck.

"We cannot go ashore until the light awakens because the gate will not open," a drowsy man told the girls, who interpreted it for me. The girls went back to bed, and the boatman was soon snoring again. I sat out on deck with the sleeping men, watching the gray light creep over the buildings which lay dark and indistinct against a gray sky. Boats anchored around us now began to assume shape and to show their colors of blue and orange, blue and red, or yellow; all of them were clean and tidy. In most of them bamboo baskets of live ducks or chickens hung over the prow, and later the girls told me people were fattening them up for the coming New Year festivities. According to the moon calendar, the Chinese New Year did not come until late January. I sat in the cool, misty dawn trying to imagine myself a little girl born on one of these boats, cooking meals in a little clay pot, rowing passengers back and forth across the river. At marriage such a girl merely transferred to another boat, gave birth to her babies on it, and reared her family there. She had no knowledge of anything in all the world except what she saw and heard on or around her boat.

At seven in the morning the day came alive. Innumerable coolies trailed along single file with trunks suspended from the poles that linked each two, while suitcases hung from the ends of the carrying pole on each man's shoulders. We three girls followed the cavalcade up wet stone stairs between high walls (that reminded me of streets in Palestine) until at last we came to an unpaved road wide enough for a ricksha. This we followed until we came to a high, iron fence which encompassed a fine colonial mansion set among tall old trees, flowering shrubs, and gay flower beds. This was the Girls' School of the Methodist Mission, and we entered its gates.

Then followed an exciting day of breakfast, tea, tiffin, and dinner with various groups of my fellow missionaries. I saw that they were all deeply engrossed in their work and very much in earnest about converting the "heathen." Almost none of them were college graduates. Among other places, I visited Magaw Hospital which had been built on beautiful grounds among wonderful old trees. Even though this hospital had asked that I be sent there (and I thought what a charming place it was), I had not come out for social life; besides, the good women in black were sending me to Mintsing, and there I would go.

That evening I had to leave to make the last leg of my journey, a trip of seventy-five miles west up the River Min. My guide was Mary Carleton, adopted Chinese daughter of Dr. Mary Carleton to whose hospital I was going. Mary was in charge of the Institutional Church in the city.

We said goodbye to the group of women standing in the warm light of their home and stepped out into rain and darkness to trudge along the high-walled street lit only by the kerosene lantern that Mary carried. I had my new painted lacquered umbrella, a bottle of boiled water, and a cloth bag containing one hundred silver Foochow dollars.

Mary warned me to be very quiet, for soldiers were said to be out seizing men to carry their burdens for them. We did not want to lose our boatmen. I shivered a little with excitement and followed her as silently as possible through the dark and rain. We went down wet stone stairs to the riverside and stood very quietly. A long, narrow boat with a bamboo roof over the middle section appeared out of the darkness; we quickly climbed aboard. We unrolled our bedding on the front deck and quickly fell asleep as the men propelled the little boat upstream. Now and then I awoke to listen to the pleasant squeak of the oars or, in shallow water, the rubbing of poles against the side of the boat. These sounds were very familiar, as though I had known this life before.

Around midnight we arrived at the Upper Bridge on the Min River. This bridge was constructed many centuries ago with such enormous stones that no one has been able to guess how they were put in place. Because it was too low for a steamer, upriver barges had to wait above the bridge for their passengers. We passed through an ancient arch and pulled up to a waiting boat. The New Year holidays were approaching, and young students returning home were packed aboard, even on the roof. Old Ching Chuang, our barefooted messenger, stood by the rail waiting to usher us to the part of the boat where he had bought a few square feet of space. The barge was alive with strange chatter. Suddenly I felt frightfully alone and alien. I was in a different world; I did not belong. I could not lift my feet to climb aboard. I stood unable to move. Mary and Ching Chuang waited.

Then a boy up on the roof began whistling "Sweet Hour of Prayer." At once I felt a tie between us, between the past and present, between my home and China, and it bound me together with all the people on the boat—perhaps with all Chinese people. I felt comforted and buoyed by old traditional attitudes of Christianity. I remembered my early childhood when Mother gathered her five children around the organ and taught us to sing "Sweet Hour of Prayer," "Come, Ye Sinners," "Abide

With Me," and others. Quickly I climbed into the boat, deeply grateful to the unknown boy on the roof above me. I wondered if he had seen me down in the shadows, frightened.

The next morning we awoke to find the old boat pushing easily up the wide clear Min River with lovely green hills rising from both shores. The men and women on the boat all wore blue cotton trousers and blouses, and they were all chatting softly in their musical tongue. Old Ching Chuang came from somewhere with a washbasin of steaming hot water, and we washed our faces while everyone looked on with interest.

Late in the afternoon the boat stopped at the mouth of a turbulent mountain stream. Here we and our baggage were quickly shifted down to a small boat. The boatmen stood at each end of it and used long poles to work our way up the rushing stream. Both men screamed excitedly as they guided our small craft up the rapid river, around great rocks which bullied the current in midstream. After an hour of this strenuous excitement we arrived at the county seat of Mintsing.

Mary and I climbed out of the boat, leaving Ching Chuang to bargain for rat boats to go up twenty miles of mountain stream to Sixth Town. We walked through a narrow stone-paved street with windowless houses and stores built right to the curb. Eventually we entered open country. Here we found the Boys' School and Mission Residence, headed for years by Mr. and Mrs. Eyestone. Mary and I climbed the stone stairs and entered the gate. The Eyestones invited us to stay the night, but I wanted to push on to see my new home at Sixth Town. Though only twenty miles away, it was impossible to continue in the evening. Boats all departed at dawn, for the road at night was made dangerous by both bandits and tigers. So we spent a delightful evening with this elderly couple who had given their entire lives to develop a school for boys in Mintsing County.

Ching Chuang called us at four the next morning, and we stepped out into a wonderfully moonlit scene. High mountains, partly hidden in mist, encircled us, while far below in a deep narrow valley a river white in the moonlight wound its way between dark, mysterious banks. This was the stream we had entered the day before. We would now follow it for another twenty miles toward its source in the high hills beyond.

Mary and I worked our way down the steep path to the river while the yells of the impatient boatmen echoed up and down the valley. Finally we climbed into a rat boat, a very long, narrow craft with a bamboo roof over its middle section and a boatman standing at each end. A young boy stood knee-deep in the icy water to steady the boat. We sat on the floor with our legs straight out in front of us, leaning our backs against my trunks.

Then we were off. The two men were bent low over their long spiked poles, forcing the craft upstream through the swishing shallow current. In places there were long stretches of quiet water with mountains painted on the clear surface. Then, as we rounded a corner, the river roared and rushed at us, tossing our boat up and down on angry waves. Up and up we pushed through swifter and more turbulent currents while the men yelled excitedly and poled desperately. Sometimes they leaped into the water to hold the boat when it began to slip back. Violently they strained their muscles, panting for breath as they worked up through seemingly impossible reaches of the torrent. Somehow I could not imagine Americans being able to negotiate such a turbulent stream.

Indeed, this was the most thrilling day of my young life. Up and up we went until we heard an ominous roar ahead. We slowly rounded a corner and came to a three-foot waterfall, green water rolling madly over and down into white foam. Dozens of boats waited here. Now I knew why the men yelled so impatiently at four in the morning. They all had to assemble at this waterfall to help each other up the cliff. Young boys stood on shore in harnesses to which were tied stout ropes fastened to the front of each boat. A crowd of men waded up to their armpits in the cold roaring water. Together they lifted the front of the first boat up over the falls while the boys on shore leaned in their harnesses and pulled with all their strength. That done, the men quickly shifted to the next boat, and thus a long line of them were moved up over the rapids.

Again came a strange feeling that I had known this life before. This was real life. In the United States we rode in cars, lived in comfort, sought pleasure, and followed our own desires. I felt that was not real living. It was an artificial existence which led only to shallow enjoyment. Here were people really at grips with down-to-earth life, yet they seemed to be getting real joy out of it. They smiled, they joked with each other, they sang as they toiled. I had now entered a way of life that was elemental and earthy and hard. This was a world where soft comfort was scorned. Here were people with a long background of rich culture and high ethical teachings, a people who had learned endurance and patience from centuries of suffering and poverty. But they sang as they worked. Their eyes were bright and observant. Their faces showed intuition.

I began to study Mary. She was a quiet young lady, a few years older than I, with gentle eyes and little wrinkles of humor around them. Her lips showed fine discipline and control; her conversation revealed straight, logical thinking, excellent judgment, and practical common sense. She was an unusually thoughtful girl. Kindness was written all over her face. I discovered, as we talked, that she was an excellent student of human nature. She possessed deep understanding and tolerance. In spite of her Ph.D. degree, she was humble. I knew I had found a valuable and enduring friend.

On either side of our stream ran little paths which served as the main highways north and south through Mintsing County. I knew that some day I would walk those paths, as well as all the other paths of the county. I would soon explore towns, villages, and tiny hamlets. In this county lived two hundred thousand people. The mission hospital to which I had been assigned in Sixth Town offered the only modern medical help to this vast population.

We passed quaint little villages. The ancestral homes were lovely, with curved roofs and ridgepoles painted in red and blue patterns. We

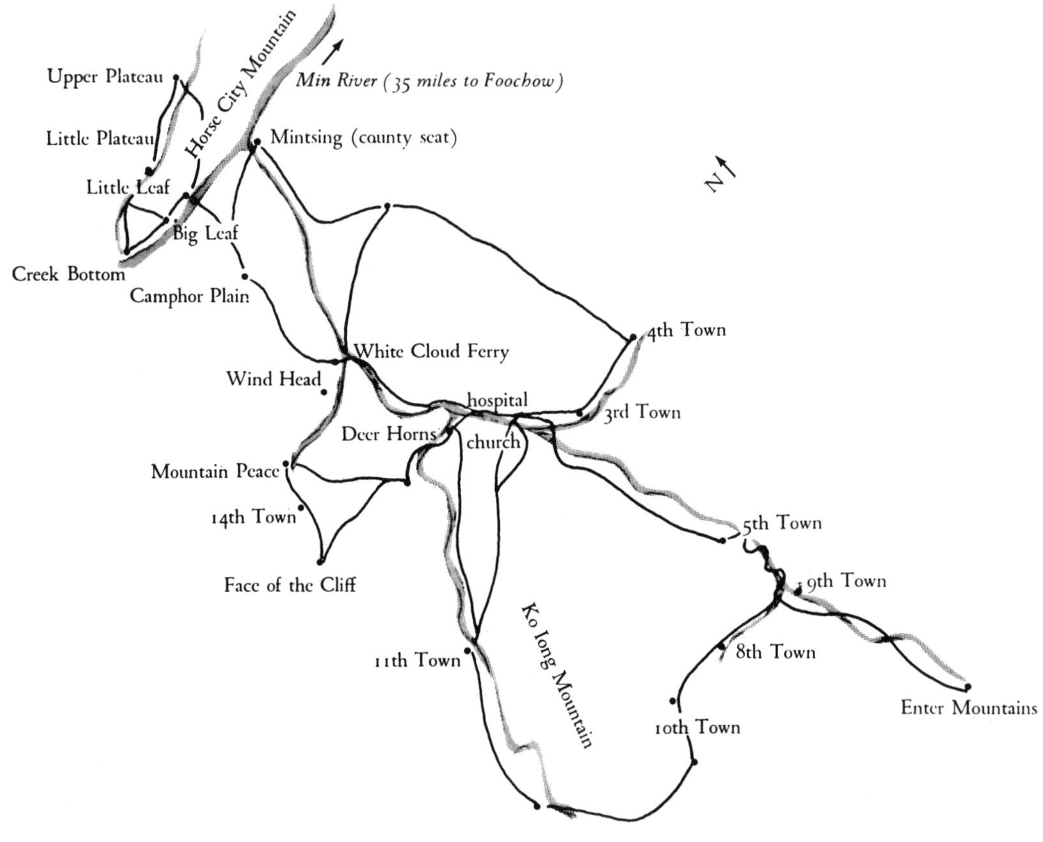

MINTSING COUNTY

Footpaths —— Rivers and creeks

Compilation of sketch maps of Dr. Hemenway originally drawn by Mary Elizabeth Shelton

saw enormous bamboo waterwheels, perhaps fifty feet in diameter, each industriously turning a log fastened to its hub. The log disappeared into a little thatched hut where, in its turning, it tripped little hammers that rose and fell on stone dishes of rice. This traditional and complex technology was used to polish rice. Other waterwheels turned a device that crushed sugar cane into syrup.

The fields on either bank of the stream were terraced for sugar cane or rice, making rich green squares all over the narrow valleys. Ominously thin yellow cows, great gray water buffalo, black pigs and goats wandered over the landscape. High mountains formed the background. House cleaning was in progress; women on their knees at the water's edge vigorously scrubbed their furniture with white sand. Other women, kneeling on flat rocks, scrubbed blue clothing. As we passed their homes we saw clothes drying, strung on bamboo poles thrust through sleeves and legs.

We saw a funeral procession led by a man carrying a red banner while another beat cymbals. A third man followed them carrying red and white streamers on a bamboo pole. Four men struggled under the weight of a heavy black coffin on which was spread a red blanket. After the coffin came neighbors and friends of the departed, attired in blue trousers and blouses. At the rear were mourners dressed in sackcloth.

Then we saw a trousseau procession. A long line of men filed along a narrow path toward the bride's new home carrying various pieces of red lacquered furniture. Mary explained that the furniture was taken the day before the wedding so that all would be settled before the bride arrived for the ceremony.

Our boat struggled up and up through Second Town, White Cloud Ferry, Fifteenth Town, and Deer Horns. After nearly twelve hours, sitting with our legs straight out in front of us and our backs against the hard trunks, we spotted a high conical peak in the west. Mary told me it was Ko Iong, just opposite the hospital. My heart was now pounding with excitement. The legs no longer ached and even the backache was gone. We were approaching my new home.

We floated around a bend and saw a long-legged bridge with no railing stretched across the stream. Not far from the right shore stood a quaint white church near the base of Ko Iong. On the left shore a little village huddled at the end of the bridge. Just beyond was a high gray-blue wall that enclosed white buildings. This was the hospital. A narrow sidewalk ran between the high wall and the river bank. A gate in the wall was capped with a little curving roof. Beside the gate, but enclosed within the wall, stood a tremendous old camphor tree that spread its ponderous branches out over the sidewalk and over a corner of the hospital grounds.

A crowd stood under the camphor tree. More people were running to join them. A slender white woman in a gray suit stood among them waving her hand to us. That was Dr. Mary Carleton who had left her medical work in Foochow in 1894 to begin work in Mintsing County. She was now old and ill, but had held on until a young doctor could come to take over. I was deeply touched by her frail condition and the thought of the many years she had labored here. Around her were a Chinese woman doctor, nurses, Bible women, teachers, preachers, servants—all of whom joined this old woman doctor to welcome me.

Their happy smiling faces and the realization that these were my future co-workers touched me deeply. I landed and scrambled up the bank. Dr. Carleton grasped my hand and introduced me to Dr. Gieu Dang, her adopted daughter, and then to the others. I had to fight back tears as I met my future comrades and entered the gate of my new home. I looked at the white hospital with its high walls, and then out through the gate across the clear stream to Ko Iong in the west, and at other mountains painted on the river's clear surface. I saw a graceful willow bending slightly on the river bank, with its delicate tassels dancing in the wind. It was a beautiful place, this new home of mine. Already I loved it.

2

The Hospital Compound

THAT EVENING we sat around an open fire. I asked Dr. Carleton why she had come to Sixth Town. She said she was so sure she wanted to give her whole life to work in China that, after graduating from medical school, she never had applied for a license to practice in New York. The Mission Board had sent her to Foochow where she worked at Magaw Hospital for a number of years. Then one day she accompanied old Dr. Nathan Sites on a preaching trip to Mintsing. In just a few days there she was besieged by over a thousand people who wanted medical treatment.

Dr. Carleton was so impressed by the need in Mintsing that she gave up work in Foochow. She moved to Mintsing with Mary, who was a small girl at the time. She had hired a few rooms in the Lau ancestral home to serve as a clinic, but conditions were primitive. The roof leaked, so when it rained, umbrellas were placed over the patients' beds.

Dr. Carleton recalled that one day a mob had gathered outside her clinic. "We know what you are doing! You tear out babies' eyes and boil them up to make your medicines!" But grateful patients then appeared and quieted the mob and she gradually won the respect of the community.

In 1894 she began building the present hospital on a tract of land purchased from the Wang clan. A strong brick building was first constructed for women patients, with living quarters for Dr. Carleton at one end. Later a typical wooden Chinese house, two stories with a veranda, was added in the rear for the nurses. An old Chinese house at the rear of the property was walled off from the nurses' home and lodged a few male patients and the male employees.

Bedtime came and "Spark Plug" summoned me to my bath. Dr. Carleton had named her this because the numerous layers of cotton coats she wore made her look like Spark Plug in the popular comic strip. Her husband, who was the cook, had been named "Barney Google."

The next morning was cold and rainy. I wanted only to sit close to the open fire, but Dr. Carleton took me through the compound. The whole area was enclosed by a fifteen-foot-high, blue-gray wall. This area was then divided into four sections with lesser walls. In the front, northerly corner—which was nearest the little huddle of shops outside and overlooked the beautiful river and western hills—was a lovely flower garden with English violets, fragrant roses, and orange, banana, and peach trees. Later, I found a guava tree in the front corner of the wall. Dr. Carleton had recently built a two-story brick building as a doctor's residence and it would soon be ready.

Through a little gate we went to the back, northeastern quarter of the compound where a very ancient and dirty old Chinese house stood. This was the dwelling for the men servants and the few male patients. It was dreadful. It contained one large, very dark room with an earthen floor, cobwebs festooning the high rafters. The beds were rough boards which had been placed across sawhorses. Each patient was rolled up in a dirty quilt brought from his home. Each had a wife along to cook meals. One man had two.

Through another small gate that was firmly locked at night we entered the other rear quarter on the south side and went through the nurses' home. In contrast to that of the men, this was a very clean two-story wooden building. It was decorated with clothes drying on bamboo poles. The nurses cooked their own meals on two Chinese frying pans in a bare little kitchen which was dominated by a big mud stove. Just outside the kitchen door were huge wooden wash tubs where each washed her own clothes. There were flowering shrubs and a big olive tree in their pleasant little yard.

Then we came to the other front section which contained the women's hospital, a long two-story, whitewashed brick building with glass windows. (Usually Chinese windows were covered with only wooden shutters.) The women patients were in antique iron beds, and they too had relatives staying with them to do their cooking. Consequently, small clay pots, the size and shape of flower pots, were scattered around the yards outside both hospital facilities. On these, family members cooked individual patient's meals over charcoal.

I had noticed that in their kitchen the nurses had one big wooden steamer which was placed on top of a big cauldron of steaming water. In the morning each nurse put her little bag of rice (marked with her name) into this steamer. At noon each quickly browned a finely cut vegetable in a little fat and simmered it in meat broth or soy sauce. Then each pulled out her bag of rice and ate it along with her personally cooked vegetable. It seemed much more delicious than our American-cooked vegetables.

As we returned to our rooms at the women's hospital building, I was already thinking that sometime we should set up a common kitchen and dining room for all the patients. Also, we would have to tear down that dreadful building out back and put up in its place a clean building which would take many more patients. Now there was not room for more than ten, but I thought we ought to plan on thirty or more. In addition, we needed an operating room, a laboratory, an X-ray, electricity, a heating system, and running water. I had never dreamed there could be such a primitive hospital in the world. The following days seemed like a bad dream. It was impossible to digest the shock of such a situation.

In the days to come I was to be further dismayed by the climate. Though I was born and brought up in New England, even that had not conditioned me for the rigors of Mintsing weather. Some days it was so cold that my hands were purple with blanched fingers, and chilblains appeared on hands and wrists, ears and nose, feet and toes. Spark Plug did all her housework with one hand because the other was holding a fire basket, a small bamboo affair which held a saucer of live coals. The climate was so damp that clothes, shoes, and books showed great blotches of mildew. Whenever it stopped raining we had to take them out for a sunning. My bones ached with the dampness.

In addition to the shock I felt on realizing the condition of the hospital, and suffering from the aching cold, I found the language barrier frustrating. It was painful to be unable to understand people and not to be understood. Weeks went by before a language teacher could be found for me. Then there was the isolation. Mintsing seemed the furthest point in the world from home. Of course, the other doctors spoke English, and in a nearby village called Eighteenth Fair, there were three missionary women who also spoke English. But that was a small number and I felt hemmed in. There was no radio. Newspapers from Shanghai arrived two weeks late. New books were rare. And how could one buy books on a salary of $700 a year in any case? There was no music except what I brought with me on the victrola. Sometimes I was seized with a frightful longing for my familiar world across the Pacific, a longing so sudden and so intense that it brought tears to my eyes.

That first day, in spite of my deep shock, I accompanied Dr. Dang on her ward rounds and then to her dispensary. This gave me an opportunity to see the people who came for help. With Dr. Dang interpreting, I began to see firsthand something of the results of the poverty and ignorance, superstition and fear, which characterized their lives. Opportunities for mental development, spiritual growth, and economic betterment seemed to me very limited. Their background was so very different from mine; there seemed to be a giant gulf between us. How was I to bridge that gulf?

One evening, as we gathered around the fireplace, Dr. Carleton asked me what I thought of her medical establishment and work. I was new in this land and unused to Chinese customs; she had been here since the year I was born. She had been trained in an early medical school, before the day of microscopes, and had done the best she could. I would accomplish nothing by expressing my shock and disappointment, and I would wound her deeply. I hesitated. Then I began very carefully, with minor things. "It does not seem safe to handle terribly infected cases without rubber gloves," I ventured. "It is unsafe for the patients, and it is unsafe for nurses and doctors."

"I suppose so," Dr. Carleton replied. "When I graduated from medical school we did not have rubber gloves, and I have gone all these years without them."

I paused and then added, "I think we ought to start with a simple laboratory where we can do urinalysis, blood counts, and smears."

"I know you must have those things," she replied warmly. "Somehow we must get the money for them." Dr. Carleton explained the difficulties she had encountered obtaining funds for medical purposes from church people who sat on committees that allocated funds; these people generally felt funds were needed more for evangelism than for medical cases. I recalled my one session with the Board. I saw that I must carry on the Bible course with great diligence, for I soon would be writing that august body in regard to our medical needs.

"We desperately need to get the windows screened," I continued, feeling encouraged to air my desires. "Those filthy flies crawl over horrible sores in the wards and then come to walk over our cooked food."

"To that I will never give my consent," Dr. Carleton said firmly. "Screens keep out the air. We have mosquito nets on our beds. But screens on our windows—never!"

"What about an operating room?" I asked, seeing my screen plan crushed for the time being.

"I have been thinking that we might whitewash the old cow barn and use that," she answered quietly, anxious to cooperate. "As for electricity, we put in a Delco plant some years ago but it will not work. We will have to get a man down from Shanghai to get it going. Then we can have electric lights."

"How wonderful that would be," I exclaimed. "Then we could have running water."

"Some years ago a friend in the States sent the Board $1,000 to set up a windmill here but I never used it. I have been thinking that we might use the money for an electric pump. We could build a water tank to hold the water and fill it each day from our wells."

Encouraged by her cooperative attitude, I went on. "Sometime there ought to be a decent building to house men patients. I wonder why they are now in such a dreadful building."

"I am glad you have thought of that," she said. "I think we can find the funds to build a proper building for them. I have been delaying, waiting for someone to take my place and carry on the work."

The cold rainy days of February 1924, slipped past quickly enough, for I found the hospital work absorbing. Dr. Dang told me stories of the patients and their backgrounds and interpreted their remarks as I saw them daily in the wards and clinic. Gradually, as I began to see and feel their environment, I began to understand them a little and to feel the bridging of the gulf between us.

One of my early patients was Mr. Wang, an elderly man who came from a village out beyond Eleventh Town. He arrived by chair with painfully swollen knees, saying he had suffered for a good many years. "I have been so lame that I am no good in the paddy fields," he said. "All I can do is mend bamboo baskets, wooden buckets, cattle yokes, or carrying sticks, as well as sun the rice. First it was one knee, but now it is both." Local fakirs and fortune tellers had treated him without success. At last he had decided to give the "Foreign Devils," as we were called, a chance to try their powers on him. He spread his dirty old quilt on a dirty old bed of ours. A nurse took his temperature.

"That is good medicine. I feel better already," he exclaimed when the thermometer was removed from his mouth.

The other men in the dim room laughed. "That is just a device to find your body heat," they explained. "There is no medicine in that glass stick."

"Nevertheless," insisted Uncle Wang stubbornly, "I feel better."

We two doctors got his history and examined him. As we left he said to the other patients, "My sickness is in my knees but they examine the whole body and ask all those foolish questions." We returned with needles to take the fluid from his knees. Then we shot some old bubonic plague serum into his knees, as suggested by a recent *China Medical Journal*.

"Is that water in my knees so precious that they carry it with them?" he asked his fellow sufferers.

"They want to examine it under the Clearly-See-Tiny-Thing-Mirror," the other men explained, laughing heartily at his ignorance. Some of them had been there a week or more and knew all these things.

I remember the day that he climbed into a chair for the long ride home. His brother had come for him and was amazed to see him walking with no pain or swelling in his joints. "Truly they are clever doctors," the brother exclaimed as he looked at Uncle Wang.

"Yes," said Uncle Wang. "They have wines for every disease."

A country woman came into the clinic with a child of ten whose abdomen was badly distended. "This good-for-nothing son of mine has had a bellyache for a long time," she shouted at us. "I tried to find some cockroach feces to feed him but could not find any. So I fed him rat feces. But he does not improve."

I noticed his wrists had been slashed and looked questioningly at Dr. Dang. "It is the custom for our native practitioners to slash the wrists to let out intestinal worms," she explained.

We kept him a few days and purged him of countless roundworms. He went home with a flat abdomen, and I made another note of the health teaching we would need to do some day in this county of two hundred thousand people.

On another morning a group of women trotted through our gateway behind a chair carrying a very sick man. Looking through the window I could see that he was a leper with edema of the whole body; one foot was completely eaten away, and swarms of flies rested on the raw stump. "If you promise to cure him in three days, we will leave him here," shouted the women in their loud country voices.

"How long has he been sick?" Dr. Carleton asked.

"Seven years," yelled all the women together.

"Then you know we cannot cure him in three days," she said gently. "If you will bring him in once a week for an injection, perhaps we can help him a little."

"It took eight hours to get here," shrieked one woman. "We cannot afford a chair every week. You must promise to cure him in three days or we will take him back home."

Obviously we could not make such a promise. The women trailed off to buy a few hot cakes for their man. Then they started the long trek back home. Some day, I thought, we are going to do something for leprosy.

A woman carried in a six-year-old girl whose genitalia were terribly gashed. "Who did such a thing to this little girl?" I demanded angrily.

"She is my daughter-in-law. I gave her just punishment," replied the woman aggressively.

It was common custom for families to take an infant girl to bring up as the future wife of a small son. It was much cheaper than buying a full-grown bride. Also, women liked to discipline and train their future daughters-in-law in their family ways. This woman had slashed the little girl with shears as "just punishment."

We took in the child for treatment and sent for her own mother. "We want you to see what that cruel woman did to your child," we told her. She was horrified. Fortunately she had enough money to buy her daughter back. But most little child-wives had no escape.

On another day the gateboy came running to us. "A blind woman has arrived," he announced breathlessly.

Dr. Dang and I went to the front gate and found a weary little old lady sitting on the sawhorse which served as the gateboy's seat. We inquired about her health and whether she had eaten. Then we asked, "Have you come a long distance?"

"Three days' journey. Three days' journey," she said proudly in her quavering old voice. Three days of walking on tiny bound feet in red embroidered cloth shoes. Three days of walking along narrow, stone-paved trails with one hand holding the shoulder of her ten-year-old grandson who had walked a pace ahead of her. Three days on her poor, aching bound feet; up and down steep stone stairs over the mountains;

across swaying bridges over the roaring mountain streams. I tried to think what it must have been like for both of them.

"Can my eyes be repaired?" she asked eagerly. She had severe trachoma.* The inflammation had inverted the eyelids until the lashes were rubbing constantly on the balls of her eyes. This constant irritation had caused swelling, blurred vision, and finally complete blindness.

"We can cure your eyes if you are willing to let us open the knife," we told her.

Her stalwart young grandson standing beside her looked anxiously at her. "She is too old," he protested. "She cannot endure to have her eyes cut."

But grandmother spoke up for herself. "I am old and without eyes. I am no good. I prefer to let the doctor open the knife."

It was a simple matter to clear up the trachoma. Then we cut out a piece of flesh from under each lower lid and stitched the cut edges together. This pulled out the eyelid and made the lashes point outward, thus relieving the irritation. Dr. Dang did this operation very nicely while I assisted. In a few days the old lady began to see a little. When the day came for her to return home, the whole staff stood under the camphor tree to say goodbye. We watched her trip off happily upriver toward her home south of far-away Ninth Town. No longer did she have to keep her hand on her manly little grandson's shoulder.

On another day a middle-aged woman came into clinic and began unwinding a long blue cotton scarf around her waist. We watched curiously as she unwound and then opened it. There, hanging from a hole in her side, lay three feet of live intestine! When she dropped it, it hung to her knees in two lengths. "Six years ago," she explained to us, "I had a big pain in my belly and our local practitioner applied heat. After a while a lump appeared here where you see this opening. Finally the intestine came out and hung to my knee in a big loop."

* A viral disease of the eye characterized by inflammation, trachoma was very common in China.

"What happened next?" we asked.

"I suffered terrible pain and half of the intestine bulged bigger and bigger. One of our women tied a hair around the middle of the loop and at last it broke in two. The intestine emptied itself and my pain was gone." She looked eagerly at us. "Can you repair it?"

"Yes, we can. But not now. If you come back in the fall we will open the knife," we told her. We had to buy instruments, set up an operating room somewhere, and train a small group of girls before we undertook this problem. The patient and the women with her went off talking excitedly about "opening the knife" to cure her condition.

Sick people rode into our hospital in chairs from all over our county, and from other counties as well. Some of them traveled for days to get to us. Others came in boats from upriver or downriver. Some, who could afford neither chair nor boat, rode through our gate on the shoulders of strong relatives. Others struggled along on their own feet. Some came moaning, others stoically silent; but all came hoping for relief, and most of them found it.

I began to lose that feeling of utter dismay at our totally inadequate facilities. Those suffering men, women, and children were a tremendous challenge to me. I had to give my best not only to heal their diseases and bring a little sunshine into their lives, but also to see in what manner I might help remove their burden of ignorance and superstition, illiteracy and fear. I looked forward to the time when we might afford a step-by-step program to improve the hospital's standards in equipment and techniques so that our whole staff might give their best in meeting the medical needs of these people.

3
New Year's Day

New Year's Day my first year in China came in the middle of February. This was the time of feasting, visiting temples, resting, and enjoying one's family. Also it was the time to parade the local deities. Each procession was heralded by the booming of firecrackers and the sound of gongs, cymbals, and flutes. The music was fascinating. It was a part of the religion of the Chinese people and I was deeply interested and intrigued. As a procession approached our gate the music was almost overwhelming in its volume. A group of men dressed in their everyday blue cotton shirts and trousers carried a heavy, bureau-like object with a mirror at its top, with incense burning just below the mirror. The object was fastened to two poles which the men carried over their shoulders as they traveled single file along the narrow path. Following this group came men bent beneath the weight of a mud god who wore a bright red robe and sat solemnly in his chair holding a fan in one hand. His mud wife followed, similarly attired.

Behind them walked a long line of young boys, dressed in red-and-white trousers, who carried huge paper lanterns also in red and white. Somewhere in each procession appeared the two devils, Tall Brother and Short Brother. The former was a boy on stilts dressed in a long gown that reached the ground. He wore a dreadful mask. The latter was composed of two boys who walked side by side within a wide bamboo frame which was covered with the appropriate gown. Women pointed out the two devils to their little children and warned them of their fate if they were not good.

The night processions were particularly beautiful, with the sweet sounds of flutes and stringed instruments coming through the black darkness, punctuated by cymbals, drums, and giant firecrackers. In the long line many people carried huge yellow or red lanterns, hanging on low-bending bamboo poles. The whole valley was bright with great lanterns hung at every gate.

As a procession would come nearer and nearer with its strange music which I loved, I would at the same time sense something ominously sinister in its undertones. Soon the local gods would ride by, partly illuminated by flickering flares, partly hidden by the shadows. A great incense burner trailed its sweet fragrance over the rest of the procession; its sweetness penetrated our hospital compound. Last of all came a long line of children who stood on their fathers' shoulders, clasping their little hands around the men's heads to keep their balance, while a strong hand pressed against the back of each to keep him from falling. Sweet music, loud noises, shouting and laughing, glowing light and good cheer, happy faces, and undertones of fearful mystery. Sometimes half-a-dozen processions were coming and going through the valley at once, carrying their gods to visit other temples, winding their way through paddy fields, and even ascending the hills around us—twisting in and out in the distance like strings of illuminated beads.

On the fifteenth of the first month, well along in February, women streamed to the temples, for this was their day. I got permission to visit a family temple near Sixth Town. In the middle of the courtyard four freshly butchered and dressed hogs straddled sawhorses. On the back of each was a dressed goat. Across the entire front of the altar a solid screen of dressed chickens, paper faces fitted over cut necks, sat in tiers on each other's shoulders from the floor to the high ceiling. Tiered cakes of all sizes and shapes abounded. These offerings of food would be taken home later to be eaten at a large family gathering. Huge red candles flamed around the courtyard, and gaudy paper decorations trimmed the interior.

A huge crowd pressed around me, curious but respectful, watching as I photographed every part of the temple except its painted mud god in his rich red robe. (I refrained from taking that most highly desired picture for fear it might be considered an insult.) Outside in the sunlight men fried cakes in small cauldrons over charcoal while others sold small clay images of their god. Here and there men gambled at small square tables. Everyone was happy and enjoying the holiday; even I enjoyed it immensely. The people were all refined and courteous to the stranger in their midst. They all seemed intelligent and observant, and I was beginning to know that they were a very intuitive people.

On my way home that day I thought there must be much fear in their lives; their religion with its hells and devils, its ghosts and spirits, must strike children dumb with fear. All adults must be deeply tinged with it. I wondered, as I walked along the narrow path on the bank of our mountain stream, if many people actually worshipped that mud god. Or did they simply regard it as a *symbol* of spiritual significance? I thought of the Catholics with their image of Mary, and of Protestants who revered pictures of Jesus. Though I could not come to any satisfactory conclusion, I was sure that these people were seekers after truth.

The next big event was the county fair, which came on the eighteenth of the first month each year. It was always held at Eighteenth Fair, a short way upriver, next to the Girls' School where the three missionary women lived. Before dawn men were trotting along beneath my windows, bent beneath heavy loads on their carrying sticks, moving toward the fairgrounds. I went over later to see. A man squatted by his wares with a small stone beside him on which to ring out and test every coin he received. Baskets of dishes had come from Eleventh Town nine miles away, on the other side of Ko Iong. Brooms made by fastening coarse twigs to a bamboo stick were on sale, as were plow handles. Piles of bamboo baskets in all shapes and sizes were found here and there. There were hoe handles, medicine roots, cakes of all kinds, brushes large and small, iron kettles and cauldrons, and cattle yokes. Some bartered their products. Others paid a few pennies for this or that, and each coin was sounded out on a stone to make sure it was not false. It was another day of true gala spirit. Everyone seemed happy, far more joyous than the people I had seen in more sophisticated fairs in my own country.

Off at one end of the fairground, Pastors Ding and Sia had set up seats and were taking turns preaching to whomever would listen. They had hung up charts that vividly portrayed the awful fate of those who indulged in wine, song, or women. I would have loved to stay to watch and listen, but I discovered that the audience paid no attention to the words of the wise. Instead they were completely absorbed in gazing at the strange foreign woman in their midst.

All too soon the New Year's holidays were drawing to a close and Mary Carleton had to return to her work in Foochow. When she climbed into the little rat boat for the trip to County Seat, I climbed in to go a short way with her. Mary was a very lovely girl whose parents had been friends of Dr. Carleton in her early years in Foochow. Both parents died suddenly, leaving four children. The oldest was married. Mary was next, and the doctor adopted her. The next two, a girl and boy, were brought up in a missionary orphanage. The girl was Dr. Dang. Mary went to high school and college in the United States and had received excellent offers for teaching positions, but she turned them down and returned to Foochow to head the program of the Institutional Church, with its kindergarten, school for children, classes for mothers, Bible classes, and evening classes for other adults.

Before we arrived at Deer Horns she called to the boatman to put me ashore. "Is it not amazing," one boatman asked the other, "that this woman rides down in the boat and then walks home without going anywhere?"

Old U Chai, our faithful servant, was waiting for me with an umbrella and followed me as I walked the winding path along the river bank toward Sixth Town. We met a man who spoke to me but I pretended not to understand because I was not yet sure of the propriety of speaking to a strange man on the way. He let me pass and then stopped U Chai.

"Who is this person?" he asked.

"This is the new doctor at the hospital."

"Where did the doctor come from?"

"From Beautiful Country."

"Is this a man or woman?"

"A woman," said U Chai, trying to push past him in the narrow path.

"How old is she?"

"I have never heard," replied U Chai.

"Is she married?"

"That also I have not heard," said U Chai pushing on past his interrogator.

A teacher had not yet been found for me, but of course Mary had taught me a good many phrases during her stay. I also listened to people talking all the time. Therefore I could make out this conversation.

U Chai had never been to school. He had grown up in a very poor family many miles up the River Min beyond County Seat. He had innate good sense, however, which blended with a courtesy and refinement that I was to find among all Chinese people. Very likely he could have recited long passages from the *Analects* of Confucius, and perhaps many of the classical plays and poems, although he knew not one character. Even the illiterate of China were shaped and molded by the literature and moral teachings which they received as part of the culture's oral tradition. U Chai had come to the hospital before my time, as a patient, and had decided to remain to work for Dr. Carleton. His father, all his brothers, their wives, and all their children had died, leaving him solely responsible for his blind old mother who still lived in the ancestral home far up the River Min. U Chai was slow but faithful; he spoke with a stutter and he always had a rag around one leg which suffered from a chronic ulcer.

Not long after Mary left, the Chinese preachers of the county came to Sixth Town for their yearly meeting, and they asked if they might call on the new doctor. In due time the preachers arrived, a group of between thirty and forty, dressed in gray cotton robes slit up the sides, with short black satin jackets and little round black skullcaps topped with a flat black button. Through the slits of their robes one could see the bottoms of white trousers pulled in tightly around the ankles. This was the usual attire of Chinese scholars.

They sat in a solemn circle around the room. Finally one of them spoke in excellent English. "I studied five years in Boston University."

"I was right near you, at Tufts Medical School!" I exclaimed. How thrilling to find another tie between America and China!

"You will have to make a speech, you know," he said. "I will translate for you."

I was horrified and felt wretched for a moment because I hated to be conspicuous. But if I had to make a speech, I would make one. I got up on my feet and said in Chinese, "I am very happy to have come to Mintsing and to meet you honorable scholars today. I wish to learn to be a Mintsing person." Then I sat down, glad it was over.

They roared with astonishment, pleasure and amusement, and clapped very loudly. Then one of them arose and made a beautiful speech saying they wanted me to come to their towns to get acquainted with their women and to heal their sicknesses. He said that he saw I would be a true friend to them all.

Not long after this we were awakened early one morning by a hum of excitement in the street of our little village, together with the hasty slamming together of store fronts and the sound of feet running this way and that. Hurrying out onto the porch I saw men, women, and children running this way and that with bundles and babies and pieces of furniture. Crowds were rushing into the church opposite us. In the street, merchants were slamming shut their store fronts. An excited murmur pervaded the compound. Spark Plug came lumbering in, all out of breath. "The northern troops are coming," she whispered in frightened tones, her pupils dilated, her face red and perspiring.

I was astonished that the coming of troops should cause such fright. Dr. Carleton explained that the southern troops had retreated to the south, further upriver from us. Now the northern army was pursuing them. The northern troops were the enemy. People were afraid they would seize local men to carry loads for them, or that they would demand a lot of rice.

Dr. Dang joined us and we all stood on the veranda watching. Soon a long line of men in gray came marching through the deserted village street and along the sidewalk between our hospital and the river. Some had been wounded and were bandaged; some looked exhausted; others were jaundiced. One man had lost an eye. Each soldier carried a heavy gun, a dagger, blanket, toothbrush, mug, umbrella, enameled wash basin, and dirty towel. The officers carried nothing and stepped along very briskly ahead of their brown-and-white saddle horses. They looked up at us as they passed. Some of them scowled and said unpleasant things in Mandarin. But one young officer stopped, pointed across at the church and made a very respectful bow to us before moving on.

Following them were the burden bearers, men who had been impressed from town to town as the army passed through. These poor men staggered along under great cooking kettles or cases of ammunition. Ropes tied around their necks or waists fastened them to their loads, to each other, and to the soldiers leading and following them. One poor man dropped from exhaustion beside the path, but a soldier beat him to his feet with the butt of his gun. The bearer then walked dizzily and caught the tail of a pony to help pull him along, but the guard whipped his wrist free. All day long they passed our hospital single file, and Dr. Carleton saw that our gate was kept locked. No one went out or came in. Late in the afternoon a group of strange-looking men in ragged, unkempt clothes passed under our veranda. "What in the world is this?" I asked Dr. Carleton.

"They are camp followers, perverts—very likely eunuchs," she said.

The next day, after the army had passed by, we opened the hospital gate. People returned home with their babies, bundles, and furniture. And thus ended the New Year's month.

4
Springtime Events

Pastor Lau from Third Town came to call on us in March and invited me to hold a clinic in his village church. We three doctors and the nurses packed two huge bamboo baskets with bottles and boxes, jars of ointment, powders and pills of all kinds, and dental forceps along with other instruments. It was less than two months after my arrival, and still I had no language teacher. Nonetheless, I decided to go and see what I could do.

Dr. Dang rode the three miles in a chair, but I preferred to walk with a boy who had come as a student nurse. Along the way he told me the names of things and I gave him their English titles. Thus, we both learned something. I looked at the fascinating countryside with narrow paths winding between paddy fields. High mountains hemmed us in on all sides and I longed to climb them for a look on the other side.

Pastor Lau welcomed us at his church, an old mud house where he lived, and set aside a good-sized room for church gatherings. He led us through a crumbling gate and gave us cups of hot tea. Then we went to work while a crowd of people, his parishioners and neighbors, watched. We set out jars, boxes and bottles, instruments and bandages on a long table in the little courtyard.

Hordes of people of all ages and both sexes began to push up to the table. We made them walk single file past the opposite side of the table. But with each patient came children and babies, sisters-in-law, mothers-in-law, and a few neighbors. Many men were present and they all shoved themselves into the front row so that they could hear all the histories and symptoms. No privacy was possible. A sick person at each end of the table shouted her symptoms to one of us doctors. She had to yell louder than all the screaming babies and shrieking relatives as well as shouting men who attempted to help her out in her narration. One baby's ears were packed with dirt. When I asked why, the young mother told me that her baby was only two years old, and she was afraid he was too young to bathe.

We saw forty or fifty patients that day, including some men who eventually deigned to consult us about their own troubles. We gave out dabs of ointment for their sores, pills for other troubles, advice for everything. We were screaming to be heard above the general uproar. Most of the afflictions were scabies, trachoma, intestinal parasites, abscesses, bad teeth, and malaria. The patients came from the families of farmers, boatmen, load carriers, carpenters, iron smiths, small shopkeepers.

As the sun began to drop behind Ko Iong we finished with the patients, closed our bamboo baskets, and started for home. I was dreadfully weary from the experience and it was a rest to walk the three miles home through beautiful scenery.

Near the end of March my language teacher appeared. He was Mr. Wu, seventeen years old, quiet, refined, and gentle. He had an aristocratic face, beautiful hands, and he dressed in the usual blue robe of cotton worn by the scholar class. "This is my first time away from home," he said pathetically. "My heart is very lonely." He was a Foochow boy and felt that he had come to a very wild and dangerous part of the world. After our first talk he said, "I must write to my wife at once. She is very troubled about my dangerous trip to such a very distant place."

The next morning I gave him a chair and a table in the hospital where he could sit all day long. Whenever there was a pause in the medical work I rushed to that table and started to learn the language. I learned that the Foochow tongue had seven tones for each syllable; each tone gave it an entirely different meaning. *Sang* in the highest tone meant "mountain," while in a tone a shade lower it meant "umbrella"; and if said with an upward slide at the end, it was the word for "name." The fourth tone went a little higher with an accent at the end, while the fifth tone started higher and dropped a little. The sixth tone seemed to start there and drop lower. The seventh was no longer used, and I felt deeply grateful for that. The eighth was the highest and the shortest. It was dreadfully discouraging to try to differentiate them.

Mr. Wu spent hours drilling me on the seven tones. It was such a relentless, unyielding exercise that I wanted to scream. It was insufferable. But it was the only way. Later he started me reading characters; that was utterly fascinating. Characters were made up of a radical which was often in the left position of the character and usually indicated something of its meaning, while a phonetic element sometimes indicated the character's pronunciation. Thus one often had two clues to what the mysterious character might be. But my teacher stood for no nonsense in analyzing characters. Chinese always memorized them and that was the only method. I might analyze by myself, but not in his classes. This gave me a sense of frustration because analysis was my natural way of studying. Always I had to learn by sheer memory here in China, and always I rebelled inwardly.

I discovered that the radical for "mouth" appeared in all words denoting eating, drinking, singing, talking, scolding, and so on. The radical for "wood" appeared in words denoting furniture, buildings, forests, and trees. The radical for "cloth" stood on the left of characters meaning clothing, bedding, cotton, silks, linen, draperies. The radical for "hand" could be found in characters which related to sewing, washing, mending, building, making, cooking, cleaning, writing, striking.

The form of sentences was very simple, so simple it was most difficult to decipher the meaning. One had to study long on each sentence in order to deduce its meaning; even then it might be interpreted in different ways.

Sometimes Teacher Wu's mind would wander and his eyes would close gently. I was not at all surprised. In fact it seemed strange he could ever come back to reality after drilling a fool foreigner on seven tones for two hours, or after struggling to imbue her brain with some dull and fleeting impression of how a character looked. However, discipline had to be maintained. When I would recite my lesson all wrong, or would skip parts of it, one of his eyes would open just a narrow slit. I suppose he saw something naughty in my face. At any rate, both eyes would fly wide open, and he would be very bright and alert for awhile. By the end of May I knew one thousand characters and also six hundred medical terms that I picked out of a Chinese book on nursing.

Two months after I arrived in Sixth Town, Dr. Carleton allowed me to go out for the evening for the first time. I went over to Eighteenth Fair for a dinner with the three missionary women who lived there. When I arrived at their gate I greeted their wizened old gateman who reminded me of the chemist in Romeo and Juliet. "How is your health?" I asked him politely.

"Very fortunate, very fortunate," he replied with a beaming smile.

"In what manner are you fortunate?" I asked, glorying in my newborn ability to understand and be understood.

"Because I am not shivering," he replied happily.

It was a raw, rainy, cold day and he was dressed in one layer of thin cotton, his feet were bare on the cold, wet brick walk, he lived on a pittance of six dollars a month, his meals consisted of unsalted rice with a bit of vegetable. But he was fortunate.

I was attired in two woolen sweaters and a heavy coat, and I shivered as I stood talking to him. I had every kind of material security. But I was not always happy. I was distressed and disturbed by the kind of religion in which I had been brought up and which was now silently surrounding me with unspoken pressure. I was very lonely in this isolated part of the world. Life was very complicated, and I had not found the answers. I was growing away from the thought that "if you believe, you will be saved." Believe what? That Jesus was born of a virgin? That the Jews were God's favorites? That Jesus died to "save" me? But even if one believed these things, how could such beliefs be the heart and core of one's religion? What was the essence of religion? I did not know. Perhaps some day I would find the answers. In the meantime my only religion was my medical work, where the need was so tremendous.

5
I Become the Patient

IN THE SUMMER of 1924 I began to have repeated attacks of fever and abdominal pain. Dr. Carleton was worried. We decided to escape the heat at Ku Liang (Drum Mountain), in the vicinity of Foochow. How wonderful to look forward to rest in cool breezes, to listen to ocean music and to feel free to study hours each day. We left Sixth Town in the middle of May with a string of four boats holding Teacher Wu, Barney Google and Spark Plug, our mountain of baggage and ourselves. I had anticipated the wonderful ride downstream, shooting the rapids we had toiled up through in January. But I was so miserable that I lay on the bottom of the boat, ill with high fever and increasing abdominal pain.

Around two in the morning our two boatmen began chanting in a minor key, alternating lines. "I have a hernia, I have a hernia," is what the front man appeared to be caroling. Then the rear one sang, "O Yo Ho La, O Yo Ho La," after which the man in front would quickly reiterate his trouble.

Later on we heard screaming and loud outcries on shore, perhaps two hundred feet from us. The boatmen leaped to their feet.

"What is that?" I asked in alarm.

"Bandits raiding a village," they said very softly. "We will not make a sound."

We were utterly silent, and the boat drifted noiselessly along. I thought of the men being murdered, of the women being raped, of helpless children being killed or savagely beaten or taken off to grow up to banditry. Poverty must be bitter in such a place, but it could be tolerated. How though would a little hamlet endure this added suffering?

Further downriver someone suddenly shouted from shore. "What is your cargo?"

The boatman answered not a word, but punched our messenger

Ching Chuang. He was equal to the situation. "A cargo of doctors," he shouted to the black night in a loud and cheerful voice.

"Go on," came the command.

By the time we arrived in Foochow I was so ill that four strong men carefully carried me on a stretcher through the streets to Magaw Hospital. There I lay motionless for a long, long time. Every movement increased the pain. I lay as still and as drowsy as a dormouse. At first I was treated as a typhoid case. Then someone found an amoeba and they treated me for that. In my silent thoughts I kept asking myself, "Why don't they treat me for malaria?" Mintsing was frightfully infested with malaria in all its pernicious and unusual manifestations. On the other hand, I thought of those flies crawling over patients' sores and then into our kitchen and on our food. It might well be amoeba. I thought a lot about those screens and tried to think how we might get them.

Dr. Carleton became desperate and moved me to Tai Maiu, the Girls' School I had visited on my arrival to Foochow in January. There I lay in a large upstairs room with high ceilings, with great windows wide open. One evening there was a prayer meeting downstairs. One missionary prayed the Lord to keep back the rain so that they could have a well-attended community prayer meeting a day or two later. Then another good woman prayed Him to send the rain to cool the suffering sick. I was one of the suffering sick lying motionless on my bed at the top of the stairs, so I silently placed my bets on her. The next day it began to pour. The suffering sick in my room enjoyed the blessed cool, but reflected that someone ought to warn that second missionary to be very careful for what she prayed. It was evident that she had influence with the listening God.

I continued to lie motionless and apparently somnolent, although my mind and ears were alert to all that went on. Dr. Carleton was deeply distressed about my condition. One day she sat by my bed and suggested taking me to Drum Mountain, where the air was fresh and cool. The next morning chair men came in with a long bamboo chair. They busied themselves putting a canopy over it and fixing two long bamboo poles to its sides with strong ropes. Then they weighed all our bamboo baskets of bedding, clothing, and food for a summer on Drum Mountain. Early the next morning our long cavalcade wound single file along the narrow streets of Foochow and then out to the winding paths of the countryside. Behind us wound a long line of blue-clad men carrying yellow-brown bamboo baskets which rose and fell with the spring of their bamboo carrying-sticks.

Fields golden with the first crop of ripened rice lay on both sides of our stone-paved path. Mothers knelt by little streams washing clothes which then were placed in red buckets. Children played naked on the ground among pigs and chickens. We met a small group of soldiers in their gray uniforms carrying long, heavy guns on their shoulders. A scholar in his white linen robe carrying a fan paced slowly along the narrow path. Many men and women in their blue cotton blouses and trousers came and went as we crossed the plain.

Now and then we passed through a small village. Houses were packed tightly together to conserve land for rice growing. Along the short street of such a hamlet stood small shops with pieces of meat hung from the ceiling, or with counters heaped high with all kinds of cakes. Other shops sold idol paper,* clothing, bolts of cloth, dishes, shoes. Here and there were tiny barber shops. In one village men were chiseling and carving gods out of blocks of wood.

Ahead of us rose a great block of mountain, dark as a chocolate cake, with an icing of rocks which glistened in the sun. After a few hours we began climbing the steep stone stairs which wound up and out of sight around great bare cliffs and through pine trees. My four chair men wore coarse white linen shorts and a long blue cotton scarf which served as a cape in cool weather, but now each man folded it under the ends of the chair poles which pressed on their shoulders.

* A missionary term for the ceremonial paper money, burned in offerings to the ancestral spirits.

On we went, laborious step by step, up and up. The air began to feel cool. The men stopped and carefully spread two woolen blankets over me as we rose high above the Foochow valley. In the afternoon we arrived. It was a stone house set by itself among very tall pines on a tongue of land surrounded on three sides by a very deep valley. The air was keenly cool and freshly fragrant. It had a wonderful effect on me. I began to have an appetite, to go to the table for meals, to even step outside on my poor weak feet. Teacher Wu came. We sat outside the door under a canopy and studied faithfully every day.

And I thought about what I was doing in China. Missionaries from various parts of the province of Fukien came to call. Over and over I was impressed by their devotion to their work, their selflessness, their utter dedication to Christianizing the "heathen." I would think what wonderfully courageous people they were, willing to die for their cause. I wondered what was wrong with me, for I could not be enthusiastic about changing a person's religion. I felt his religion might be as good as mine in many ways, and even better for him. I did not go to China to tear down a person's faith in what he had found for his security. But I did want to bring him healing, to somehow help him discover some of nature's laws of physical, mental, and spiritual health which would enable him to bring up his children with better opportunities. That was the truth I could bring him, at least to the extent that I, myself, had answers. And there was much that we could learn about life from the Chinese.

My fever returned and the abdominal pain came with it. Again and again this happened. I thought of all the atypical cases of malaria I had seen in Mintsing during the three or more months there, and in desperation I began to dose myself with quinine. It worked. Soon I was strong again.

Now it was possible to visit other missionaries, to go to church, parties, and picnics. On one picnic we passed through mountain-top fields of rice, sweet potatoes, peanuts, and tea trees. We met men and women sweating under heavy loads of wood, charcoal, and rice. One woman balanced a great log across her shoulder, and we wondered how she had hoisted it in place.

The picnic area was among huge, black boulders. We sat on the ground and looked down into a deep valley with a tiny winding river and a microscopic village on one bank. Tiers of mountain ranges in lavender, shading off in the distance to permanent blue and then faintly gray-blue on the horizon, stretched away into the sea.

Teacher Wu and I studied every morning, and while we worked curious men gathered around in respectful silence until we finished. Then we closed our books and looked up to see beautiful old embroideries spread out around us, lacquered boxes, vases of marvelous cloisonné, amber beads, jades and other jewels, pure silver things, laces of all kinds. These beautiful things gave me great respect for the artistic quality of the Chinese people. These people loved beauty in nature, music, painting, literature, and gentle manners. But I bought very little. How could it be right to put my money into these things when people were starving all around me? How could I indulge my whims when my fellow creatures had nothing? I compromised by buying a few things for Christmas presents.

In early September Dr. Carleton felt I was well enough to start back to Mintsing. She wanted me to go down to Foochow to live with Mary Carleton a few days to see how I fared at sea level before she dared to take me back to Mintsing.

Another missionary and I took mountain chairs down to the city. Then we rode in rickshas through the narrow, winding streets. We crossed the Bridge of a Thousand Years and met a few little horses wearily tugging heavy, awkward carriages. When we passed a row of attractive looking houses, my companion called to me, "Those are Bad Houses." Of course I looked with renewed interest and noticed a long line of rickshas and carriages waiting in front of them.

We dashed through the dark Water Gate into the city proper, where the streets were paved with long stones worn by centuries of passing feet. We whirled into Jade Street, with all its shops of jades and flower vases; and then around a corner into Pawn Street, where the shops were filled with used clothing. Here and there a dreadful beggar man or woman in rags lay moaning in a gutter holding an emaciated baby. Further on we saw small boys hard at work in the open fronts of carpenter or smith shops. Huge red banners with shop names floated gracefully over the streets and lent a bright dash of color to the scene.

Darkness came on and there was only a faint light here and there as we rushed through high-walled, narrow, and winding streets. Here was a dim Chinese paper lantern high over a street; there a flickering candle at a fruit stand. Through a temple door I caught a glimpse of silent, serious people standing before a gilded altar in the light of flaming torches. Cymbals and skin drums added mysterious sounds to the rites. We finally turned into aristocratic South Street and quickly arrived at Mary Carleton's outer gate.

In 1915 this home, which had been built on elaborate scale by a high official, was turned over to the church to be used as a family center. Now it was the "Church of the Higher Friendship," a Christian social center. Mary took me to see the libraries and reading rooms for parents, sewing and cooking classes for young women, a kindergarten for fifty youngsters, primary and grade schools, baths for babies. In the evening they offered good movies and lectures to an average audience of six hundred. Fifty apprentices were studying in the night classes, while one hundred and fifty poor children were being given instruction in a daily Bible school. Mary managed all this with a quiet calmness and humor.

While in Foochow, Mary took me on outings to the Buddhist monastery on Drum Mountain and to the city's Confucian Temple. On another occasion we went to see a government orphanage. This politically managed institution was in shocking shape, and Mary and I longed to take it over, build it up, and give those unwanted, desperately neglected babies a chance to grow into useful citizens. What a wonderful opportunity for those in charge, and how sorely was it missed because of greed and indifference. I would have given my entire life to such a project.

Soon however our messenger, Ching Chuang, arrived from Mintsing, and Dr. Carleton came down from the mountain. Then we started upriver on a large boat carrying new furniture for my room and big supplies of new drugs and groceries. On the second day I was lying quietly with a fever when Ching Chuang suddenly slid down into the interior, his eyes bulging. "Bandits! Bandits! Go show yourselves quickly." What a strange request. But his urgency persuaded us to act at once and ask later. Dr. Carleton and I climbed out on deck while the rest cowered inside. There stood two armed bandits on shore staring at us. Four more came to join them. They looked us over and signaled the frightened boatmen to be on their way.

"Why did they want to see us?" Dr. Carleton asked the messenger.

"They asked me what my cargo was and I said it was a cargo of unmarried girls. But they insisted on seeing whether or not I was deceiving them," our old rogue explained. What he had actually told them, we could not guess.

That night as I lay on a mattress on the boat floor I went over the past interesting days in Foochow. I pondered over the fact that men created beauty of design and line, and beauty of color and finish in the Buddhist and Confucian temples; that all around the world men put beauty into their great cathedrals. At the same time they settled their disputes by slaughtering their fellow men. I was convinced that the heart of religion must be very intimately and vitally a part of human relationships; otherwise, of what use was it? There could be no meaning or value to anything called religion without a central thought of service. Service must be the essence of religion. But there must be more. I thought it must be a belief in man, in his great and wonderful possibilities; a belief in a heaven on earth if we would live in the right relationships. But there was even more than that. I was looking for something mystical with which to integrate this belief in man, this ideal relationship. More than that I could not see. And I seemed to be very much in the dark as I lay there in that boat that night on my way back up the River Min.

6

Autumn Activities

IT WAS OCTOBER 1924, a month of blue and gold. The deep blue creek wound in and out among golden rice fields and past little huddles of villages brooding under spreading camphor trees. It was the month when blue-clad farmers applied their sickles to the ripened rice, whacked the stalks over a kernel box to receive the rice seeds, stacked the rice stalks in shocks like our corn in New England, and then carried home their big bamboo baskets of kernels. Their women would spread the rice out on bamboo mats in the courtyard for a number of sunny days until it was dry enough for the polishing mill. All day long and through the night, I could hear the thump, thump of the revolving log turned by a waterwheel. The ponderous log tripped a row of little hammers as it turned, and they rose and fell rhythmically, striking the kernels again and again until they were polished.

October also brought the cormorants. Each man sat on his tiny raft of three bamboo poles tied together with vines. A big bamboo basket was placed right behind him, and three black cormorants sat in a row along the raft. Each bird had a long rope tied to one leg and a band fitted over its neck. I loved to watch the man sitting leisurely on an upturned basket in the middle of the raft while the shining black birds took turns plunging into the water with a big splash. A bird would return quickly with a large fish in its mouth, which it could not swallow because of the ring around its neck. The master's hand would shoot out quickly, seize the fish, and hurl it into his basket. From time to time he removed the rings and let his birds eat a fish or two.

This was the month when we bought stove wood for the coming winter. We awoke one day to see a long yellow snake lying on the surface of our river. This snake was made of medium-size peeled logs tied end to end. Then stove-length wood came floating leisurely downstream, until by sunset the river was full. The wood sellers now arrived and plunged into the water up to their armpits, using long wooden rakes to guide the wood to shore. When it rained, a man would hold an umbrella over himself with one hand and rake with the other. Someone else in a small boat cruised around shepherding in stray sticks not reached with the rakes. When the wood had been landed the men quickly built a little house of it, leaving an open space for a door. There they lived and cooked their meals over a small clay pot until the wood was sold. We bought our winter supply at the rate of 280 pounds per dollar. Dr. Carleton delayed buying for several days, waiting for the wood to dry out and become lighter. In the night, however, I heard the men under my windows pouring water over the wood to keep up its weight.

Developing the hospital was a very exciting event that first autumn of 1924. We bought rubber gloves and ordered laboratory equipment. We prepared a little room for a laboratory and we whitewashed the old stable for a temporary operating room. Surgical instruments were already on their way to us. We took in a few boys to train along with the girls, expecting them to pass the national examinations at the end of three years and thus get national nursing certificates.

We carefully interviewed each boy to see what he was like and what were his possibilities. I took pains with those boys. I taught them to do things that they found interesting. I dissected a frog to demonstrate its inner workings and to give them some dim idea of human physiology. I hunted up pictures to illustrate their lessons. Before long Dieu Hok, son of a pastor, learned how to pull teeth. The day came when I let him pull one all alone without my supervision. It came out well and he giggled delightedly to himself and said under his breath, "The first time! The first time!" But not all events were so propitious.

One day I found that a dressing had not been changed and I asked him why. "I thought tomorrow would do just as well," he said naively. Truly, much more had to be learned.

When the laboratory apparatus arrived, we set it up in our newly painted little room. At that time a young student named Stephen Lau came to work in the laboratory. Stephen was a bright boy of sixteen with a smiling, happy face. He was a quiet and gentle boy, and unusually thoughtful. He loved animals and all growing things.

When he was six years old, his widowed mother was a cook at the hospital. She provided the only support for her mother-in-law and two children. Stephen's mother lived at the hospital while his grandmother looked after the two boys in the ancestral home. Once when Stephen became ill and his grandmother called in native doctors and fortune tellers to treat him, Stephen would have nothing to do with them. At last his grandmother asked him what to do. He was the older son and the future head of the house, so this was quite proper, in spite of his youth. "If you want me to get well," Stephen said, "call Church Aunt over from the hospital." Apparently he had had chats with this elderly lady with bound feet—matron of the hospital—when he went to visit his mother. He had felt her love and wisdom. Soon Church Aunt was trudging across our shaking bridge on her poor bound little feet, leaning on her stout staff as she moved step by step along the rough, stone-paved path. Church Aunt persuaded Stephen's grandmother to send him to the hospital for treatment. He eventually recovered from typhoid fever.

Later Stephen's mother also fell ill with typhoid, but Grandmother this time insisted that she go home for treatment by native methods. There the mother died. This left Stephen responsible for a little brother and an old grandmother, with a rice allotment from the family fields for only one person. Grandmother divided the one portion of rice between the two boys, while she drank the rice water. She became thinner and weaker as the months went by. One Sunday morning, during church service, there was a sound of feet clumping down the aisle to the front seat where Dr. Carleton sat. It was seven-year-old Stephen leading his little brother. Stephen threw himself on the floor in front of her and beseeched her to save them, weeping long and bitterly.

Dr. Carleton adopted Stephen and raised him, and she sent his little brother to trade school. The grandmother, weakened too long by starvation, died. When older, Stephen went away to high school, but because of political troubles the school had to close, so Stephen came home.

First I taught Stephen to make blood smears for plasmodium, the malarial parasite. He asked the nursing staff for their blood, and they were thrilled to have it taken and examined. He spent hours making beautiful drawings of what he saw under the microscope. He became quite expert in a short time and could distinguish the various types. He found both quartan and tertian in my blood.* That mastered, I taught him urinalysis. Later we worked on the recognition of parasite ova, roundworms, pinworms, and hookworms. Stephen was enthralled with his new knowledge and quickly imparted it to the students, who were equally fascinated. Even the children begged him to do tests on them. I wanted to teach him to grow cultures, but we lacked the equipment. But I did write a simple illustrated textbook for him on vaccines, antitoxins, various kinds of bacteria, and so on.

Life at the hospital had shifted into higher gear. Morale was high and patients were coming in larger numbers. More serious cases came to us, and I was glad we now had an operating room. Third Aunt came walking in through our gate, having come nearly twenty miles from her home in the mountains out beyond Fourteenth Town. She was very thin and weak and had an enormous goiter.

"I have been unable to eat anything but rice water for three months," she told us. "This thing on my neck grows bigger and bigger so that I cannot swallow any food. Also I have been unable to lie

* Tertian malaria is characterized by fever paroxysms every 48 hours, while quartan fever occurs every 72 hours.

down for three months. I have to sleep sitting in a chair with my head on the table in front of me."

Later on Dr. Carleton, Dr. Dang, and I met to discuss her case. "We ought to operate," I said. "She will die if we do not."

The other two looked at each other and shook their heads. "If you lose this case, there will be no more surgery," they warned me.

I had always followed Dr. Carleton's wishes, but this woman's life was at stake, and I felt I could help her. "I feel that I must try, if Dr. Dang is willing to help."

We did that operation with the entire staff standing around looking gloomy and unhappy. Dr. Dang was troubled and anxious. They were all concerned for my reputation. I made the incision, exposed the enormous thyroid, and merely tied off the big blood vessels going to it. The patient went through this very nicely, so a few days later we completed the next stage which was to remove much of the gland. It was enormous and had pushed down below the clavicle. It was very difficult to remove. However, after a few tries it came. It showed a papular growth and was probably a cystadenoma.* Despite the tremendous bleeding, we managed to sew her up properly.

It was rewarding to see the light come back into the nurses' eyes when we took her out of the operating room still alive. Of course we watched her carefully for violent reactions, but there were none. She recovered rapidly and gained ten pounds in the next seven days. It was a blessing for her to be able to swallow solid food and to lie flat on her back. On the fourteenth day she said goodbye to us and began her long walk back home. I never saw her again, but a few years later I was told that she was living and well.

Not long after that, Ninth Aunt came walking in with her intestines still wrapped in the blue cotton scarf. "Will you now open the knife?" she asked eagerly.

We cut off all the intestine hanging outside her abdomen; then

* A tumor, usually benign, of glandular origin and marked by a cystic structure.

an inch more off each end within the abdomen. I hoped this left clean bowel to make the connection. We sewed the two cut ends together and dropped it into her abdominal cavity, leaving a tube to drain through her side for a while. Ninth Aunt had a very stormy convalescence but did live through it. Because a fortune teller had told her she would die on the third day if she remained in the hospital, sick as she was, her family took her home. But after the fatal day had passed without fatality, they brought her back to us. Eventually I removed the tube and told her the opening might close in by itself in time. If it did not close in, she should return in six months and I would try to sew it closed. She, too, never returned, but we were told by relatives that she was alive and well some years later.

"You are now famous," the nurses said to me shyly after these two had gone home in good health.

7
Travels with a Pony

It was February 1925, just one year since I had arrived. We all stood under the camphor tree looking downriver for the arrival of Mary Carleton's boat. She was coming back from Foochow for New Year's. But something else excited us too. Dr. Carleton had asked the committee for permission to buy me a pony. And also a typewriter. With a pony I could travel all over the district, and with the typewriter I was supposed to write missionary letters. A friend of Mary's in Foochow had found a good pony for me, so it now would arrive with her. Needing some riding clothes, I had asked Dr. Dang. She thought I would appear less conspicuous riding through the country if I wore Chinese clothes. Also, people would be sure I was a woman if I wore the clothes of a Chinese woman.

The next day we had gone to the local shop to find material.

Village women gathered around to watch and to comment. "Do those foreign women know what kind of cloth they want?" asked one. "Are they going to use Chinese cloth?" asked another. "What do they want of our cloth? . . . They had better use their own kind of cloth. . . . What do they want cloth for, anyway?" These and many more remarks were passed as we chose a coppery-brown material to make a Chinese woman's blouse and stout, black cotton cloth for a pair of Chinese-style pants.

That same afternoon Ho Sieng came stumping in on her bound feet to make the clothes. She was a poor woman of such low status that she found it hard to get enough to eat. Long before my coming to Sixth Town she had been the sewing woman for the three missionaries at Eighteenth Fair, and her earnings there had been a great help. But one sad day the missionaries discovered that she had been sewing on Sunday, so they discharged her for not living like a Christian.

I worked on Sundays patching up ailing bodies and saw no reason why she should not patch clothes on Sunday. So she had come stumping into my garden with her face glowing because she was needed, and because she needed money. Dr. Carleton and Dr. Dang came over to help work out the problem of making clothes without a pattern. Others joined in the discussion. How to make Chinese clothes to fit a big-framed American woman who possessed a very non-Chinese shape? When the garment finally was produced, they all thought I looked much better than in my western clothes.

That had been some time ago. Now we stood under the great camphor tree and scanned the river toward Deer Horns looking for Mary's boat. Suddenly there was a strange commotion on the village street, and a crowd gathered. Then we spotted a beautiful Mongolian stallion, marked like a pinto. He pranced up to our gate. All the staff and servants dashed out to see him. He was white with brown spots at both ends and on both sides, with a thick curved neck, short restless ears, a short-cropped mane, and a long forelock over very bright eyes. Though he had just traveled twenty miles from the county seat carrying his *mafoo,** he looked fresh and spirited as he lifted his dainty hooves over our gate step.

That first medical tour with the pony was memorable. Not long after the pony's arrival we went on our first traveling clinic. Nurse Fragrant Sister went in a chair, Stephen went on foot, and I rode Patter, as I had named him. I loved the patter of his feet as he trotted along our little paths, so it seemed an appropriate name. There was a steady downpour when we started off on our trip; the road was sticky with wet clay. Patter pushed on courageously and cheerfully. A few miles downstream, as we skirted a bluff high above the rushing river, we noticed two rat boats dashing madly in the flood. As they approached a bridge, because the water was so high, one boat became caught on the underpinning. Slowly the fragile bridge began to fall into the river. The wildly careening boat went over, and we saw the two boatmen thrown into the river. The second boat came swooping down to the rescue and a man held out his pole and pulled one man to safety. The other disappeared. The rescue surprised us since the people in this region seldom attempted to save someone who was drowning.

When we came down from the high path to the riverside, some miles below the accident, we found a bridge to cross. The high bridge shook and swung rhythmically as the high water thundered against it. I dismounted Patter and we started to cross. Halfway across he stopped, snorted wildly, rolled his eyes in fright, and plunged into the river. The mad stream bowled him over and over downstream while we stood staring in horror on the shaking bridge; but just before the river turned a corner, it washed him up on the opposite bank, and he climbed ashore and returned to my call. Then we climbed up wet, slippery stone stairs and pattered along clay paths that separated paddy fields, slipping again and again. Eventually we arrived at the home of Teacher Sia, now retired, who had been the Chinese teacher at the hospital when I first arrived.

* Lit., "horse-man"; a Chinese groom.

He was pleased to see us, receiving us in the little courtyard where the women of his household brought us tea. Then we entered polite conversation. "Is the Honorable Teacher well?" I asked.

"Very well, thank you."

"Can the Honorable Teacher sleep well?"

"Yes, I sleep well."

"Does the Honorable Teacher find that he has enough teeth to enjoy his meals?"

"Thank you, thank you, I am eating well."

"Are the sons of the Teacher well?"

"My miserable sons and grandsons are all well, thank you."

After this he too inquired about my health—but not about my teeth for I was not venerable. The preliminaries concluded, we then discussed Dr. Carleton's planned return to America and other matters. At last we rose to leave, and he followed us to his outer gate. "Walk slowly, walk slowly," he said, smiling as he stood there.

"Please enter your house," we said as we bowed to him.

Then we continued our wet, slippery journey to the little hamlet where the sick were waiting for us. Fragrant Sister and I pulled teeth, applied dressings to sores and wounds, vaccinated, and passed out medicines. Finally all had been attended to. Then the local pastor invited us to a simple Chinese meal—steaming hot rice with a little vegetable and a bit of pork. After dark more sick people filed in and Stephen, chatting pleasantly with the patients, held the kerosene lantern for us as we worked.

After many hours of bawling children, yelling men, and shrieking women, I was glad when bedtime finally came. But I was equally glad when dawn appeared, for my bed—boards laid over a sawhorse up in the belfry of the local church—proved to be very cold. Having been resuscitated by a hot breakfast of watery rice, cooked like a cereal but without salt or sugar or anything else, our medical team plodded through the rain to the next little village where we vaccinated and treated for various maladies. Then we again climbed mountains over steep stone stairs. Because the pony weighed less than seven hundred pounds, I worried that my weight might be too great a burden for him on the stairs. My knees ached from the long climbs up and down. That night we stayed with another pastor in his church, where we saw sick people and vaccinated others.

What adventure! In one mountain village we were entertained by a cultured woman and her beautiful children. She was no country woman; attired in a silk dress, she wore the long nails of the leisure class. The sick in this village came pouring in as usual and there was the customary racket of crying and yelling. Suddenly, while I was interviewing the next patient, a silence pervaded the room. After the man I had been talking to left I asked Stephen what happened. Had I said something wrong?

"No," he said in a low voice. "Everyone was silent because that was a bandit that you were treating. He was among those who raided Tenth Town last night and slaughtered so many people."

While I stood in silent shock, the local pastor approached and asked in a low voice whether I would be willing to treat other bandits. "We treat sick people regardless of their reputation, occupation, or lack of virtue," I replied, also in a low voice.

Soon after this bandits came pushing into the room. They were jaunty young fellows, faces smiling, with wicked revolvers hooked into their belts, but they were very polite to me and bowed very low. One had been shot through the cheek and another through a leg; the others had less severe complaints. Now it was becoming clear that this was a bandit-controlled area and that the women and children belonged to one of their leaders.

On our way to Ninth Town we had to cross a roaring full river on a "horse-tooth" bridge. This bridge consisted of a row of tall, narrow stones set on end in the river bed, the top of the stones well above the water level. Now, because of the level of the swollen stream, they barely showed. To cross, people had to skip from one stone to the next. No one had dreamed of a pony traveling through when the bridge had been set, but we knew that an army with ponies had passed through here the previous year, so there had to be a way for ponies to cross.

I stepped boldly out on to a horse tooth, leading Patter into the water. He came meekly, with his ears laid back. It was deep enough for him to swim and all went well until we were halfway across. Suddenly he was thrown over on his back; one foot caught in the stones. I jumped into the cold water to help while Stephen called to a nearby farmer. The man came on the run, and somehow we managed to free the foot.

We arrived in Ninth Town cold and wet. Again we barricaded ourselves behind a long table in the church; patients filed in front to describe their complaints. "Speak louder," someone would yell from the rear of the room. No one wanted to miss a word. Sometimes a friend or relative would have to yell out the symptoms for a patient whose voice was too weak or whose memory was too poor. Among the afflictions were scabies, trachoma, eye infections, malaria, intestinal parasites, and tuberculosis. We treated sixty-five people in Ninth Town that day, urging some to go to our hospital for better and more extensive treatment. Then we vaccinated thirty-five more and headed for Tenth Town.

Tenth Town was much higher in the mountains than Eighth or Ninth Towns. It took several more hours of steep climbing to arrive at this hamlet. It, too, had recently been raided by bandits. Several houses had been burned and a number of people killed. It seemed likely that this village was attacked because the people would not, or could not, pay the exorbitant military taxes demanded of them by local warlords. People came to us from all over the high country of Ko Iong, and we treated 120 besides vaccinating 54 others. Here too were a number who needed further care in the hospital, so we urged them to go down to Sixth Town.

The next day we headed for a hamlet even higher up the mountain, traveling for fifteen miles on a narrow path that skirted a deep chasm. The footing was treacherous. Bitterly cold rain soaked our clothes, but we slogged along until we reached an old house that served as a school. The two men who ran this school quickly swept out a room for us and began to prepare a meal. While they cooked, Stephen took Fragrant Sister and me across a frightening suspension bridge to see a paper maker working at his craft.

"My family has made paper here for many generations," he told us with pride. Water poured through bamboo pipes from a hill above to fill his great wooden tubs. In one tub bamboo was soaking. In another stewed a certain kind of leaf. The leaf secreted an oil which was used in the first tub to break up the bamboo fibers. This would leave a thick, yellow paste in the tub. The man then dipped beautiful wire-like screens, made of very fine bamboo strips, into this paste to form a wet sheet of paper. This wet sheet was then removed from the screen and pasted on the mud wall of his furnace. The wall was covered with drying sheets. Mountain ferns provided the fuel. "One firing of these ferns gives enough heat to dry three sets of paper sheets," he said. I was fascinated with this centuries-old example of Chinese technical skill.

Next door was an herb shop. The old proprietor invited us inside, so we sat on sawhorses and chatted for a few moments. He offered us his long pipe and was bewildered that I did not smoke. (I thought of the American Indian offering his pipe and wondered if I should take a whiff for the sake of politeness.) But since neither Stephen nor Fragrant Sister accepted the invitation, I felt my breach of etiquette could not be too shocking.

Next morning just after dawn we started up the steep mountain stairway that led to Twelfth Town. After a long climb we came to the spring that was the source of the stream that cut through Sixth Town, the mad river we had crossed so many times to get to Ninth Town. In the deep valleys below us, farmers shouted to their neighbors that a foreign woman and pony were coming. Soon the bamboo groves were alive with people who ran to see us. The pony was an even more interesting sight than I, for the people had never seen one before. Of course, a foreign woman was a curiosity; but after all she was a human. "He has eyes," one shouted in excitement. "He has ears," yelled another one. "Can he hear? . . . Does he understand Chinese or English . . . Can he eat?" were some of the questions put to us. But these people were cordial and courteous and asked us into their homes. We were invited into one house for tea, but there were no cups. A grandfather-size teakettle, sweating in a thick, wadded jacket, had been placed on the bare table in a wooden bucket. Everyone took a drink from the spout.

At last we reached the top of Ko Iong range. From here on a clear day one was supposed to be able to see Foochow, seventy miles away. But if I thought the trail up was a terrible climb, it was because I did not realize what was ahead. The other side of the range dropped sharply, and the stone stairs went down at an even steeper angle. My knees became so weak that we had to make frequent stops, and Patter became so disgusted that he whirled around and started running back up the trail.

After ten hours of strenuous travel we arrived at the church of Mr. Lau Heng-tong, who was astounded to learn we had crossed the high mountain—and with a pony at that. We were exhausted. But we pulled out our medical equipment and treated the crowds of ailing people until dark: vaccinating, pulling teeth, listening to histories yelled above the hubbub, examining, and prescribing.

The following morning at dawn we headed down Twelfth Town valley. In an hour or two we came to a tiny village where people asked us to treat their sick. The women brought me a sawhorse to sit on, and they all stood around me on the street. Because I wore a Chinese woman's blouse they were not afraid of me. They smoothed my hands, admired my hair, and said all manner of flattering things.

Then, to our surprise, Uncle Wang, whose legs we had treated at the hospital, appeared. He pulled out a second sawhorse and stood on it to deliver a testimonial to my virtues, real or imagined, to the crowd. "My knees were cured by this honorable doctor. Now I can even climb a ladder," he shouted. Then he brought out a ladder, stood it up against a shop front and climbed it. Ancient bubonic plague serum injected into his knees had wrought the miracle.

In the next small town we stopped to watch a candlemaker at work. Big baskets of waxberries squatted outside his shop waiting to be taken in. Hundreds of white candles hung from the ceiling inside. A great iron cauldron sat over a fire maintained at fever pitch by a bamboo blower, tipped with tin. The candlemaker blew through the tube to stimulate the blaze of burning ferns. He would then take a strong straw and dip it in the boiling white wax made from berries before hanging it up to dry. He showed us the red coloring he used for red candles. "My ancestors made candles here for many hundreds of years," he said proudly as he worked. Of course we complimented him on his skill, and for being so filial in carrying on the craft of his ancestors.

On the crest of a hill nearby, a red resthouse stood by the path. This house also served as a modest temple. Around the altar were gathered gorgeous paintings in red and blue of dragons, tea cups, clocks, and a few other useful objects. Though in Mintsing in those days we knew time only by a sun dial, someone obviously had been to the outside world to see clocks, which now were depicted in this isolated place. The god sat placidly among these decorations even though his mud arms had crumbled away and his legs were disintegrating.

"Busak is ill," I remarked, hoping to learn the people's feelings toward their god.

The two chair coolies and a few others standing around laughed. "Please doctor, repair his illness," one of them said quickly.

At Eleventh Town we visited the sick, did our vaccinating, and gave short talks on health and disease prevention. In the future such talks would play an increasingly important role in our work.

Before the dew was off the grass the next morning, we started for Sixth Town by way of a china factory. At this factory we found perhaps a thousand people living in low thatched mud houses huddled closely together. The dishes were made in open-front huts. In one hut a man threw a handful of clay on the central tower of his revolving circular platform. He shaped the bowl roughly and completed the shaping with his hands and a little stick. In the next hut the bowls were scraped and polished as each piece whirled around on its wheel. Close to the ceiling of each hut, rows of narrow boards held bowls waiting to be painted and baked. In a large open building women were painting bowls and plates while their children played on the earthen floor. Nearby stood mud kilns with narrow doors. Many of the workers stopped to tell me their troubles, and we held a clinic right there in the factory street.

We returned to Sixth Town by a trail over the low northern end of the Ko Iong range which we had crossed and skirted for the past week. Patter had carried me faithfully over difficult trails. He had fallen over in the water, he had fallen off a bridge—he had even fallen over a water fall—and many times he had fallen down into paddy fields, but he had kept plodding along with courage. Thus, I first entered the vast field of medical need in the surrounding villages with my trusty Mongolian pony.

8

Typhoon and Little Thunder

LATE IN MAY 1925, Dr. Carleton had stood under the great camphor tree in the hospital yard for the last time. She gazed at the mountains which cupped our narrow valley with its tiny village and beautiful clear mountain stream. Then she had stepped into the boat that would take her away forever. She was going back to America in retirement. After three decades in Mintsing, it seemed a cruel fate for her to go back to a country she no longer knew.

Farewell speeches and feasts had been given in her honor. Gifts had been presented, ranging from eggs and chickens to scrolls inscribed with words of appreciation and respect, or scrolls of famous paintings. Old ladies who had been her patients and friends for thirty years visited. All the teachers, Bible women, and preachers came to pay their respects. I wondered how she could endure the heartache of her departure. In Mintsing her life had meaning, and she had friends.

We left for Drum Mountain, where she could rest above the blasting heat until a steamer put in at Foochow. Dr. Carleton was old and frail, and alone with her heartache. There was no way I could thank her enough for all she had done to launch me in my difficult work. She had stayed over an extra year, in spite of poor health, because of my illness the previous summer. In our short year and a half together she had taught me much about Chinese customs and ways of thinking; that was invaluable and would affect the rest of my life. Too soon she and Mary Carleton left Drum Mountain. Stephen was overcome with grief, for she had raised him with great love.

When we returned to Mintsing, there were a number of patients who needed operations. We did them at dawn during the next two days. One was an old lady with a cancer of the breast, and I did a radical operation on her. I knew it was too late to prevent metastasis, but it was such a foul thing that the family could not stand her in the house. Now she could go home and feel welcome for the rest of her life. We did her under ether anesthesia, an entirely new method for our staff.

Because I had promised the people at Magaw Hospital in Foochow that I would return to relieve one of their doctors, I again made the trip down rugged mountains to the Min River and finally out to the coast. In some ways life in Foochow was delightful. I loved working in a more sophisticated hospital, and it was interesting to visit with the Foochow patients, who represented such a variety of backgrounds. It was pleasant to shop in the bazaars of Foochow, and it was pleasant to meet the other missionaries in the city. But I had not gone to China for pleasure. Mintsing kept calling me back.

Though I no longer accepted the religion of my childhood, I had become certain that one's religion must be securely interwoven with service to others. In Mintsing the need for medical care was urgent. And I found that I was irresistibly drawn to the people of Mintsing who were so largely untouched by the outside world. I wanted to know more of what they thought and felt and how they did things. In a city like Foochow, missionaries had a rather superficial relationship with the Chinese people. They appeared to be endlessly trying to carry their American way of life to these people, convinced that this was their message. Unfortunately, few of my missionary acquaintances here saw the need to seek out Chinese points of view just as earnestly as the Chinese were studying our ways and customs. If a bridge of friendship were to be constructed as a link between two peoples, between two cultures, that bridge had to carry two-way traffic.

But I carried on at Foochow until the return of the doctors I had relieved. Also, I had been waiting for the arrival of Dr. Huang, whom I had first met while interning in Philadelphia. Dr. Huang had offered to relieve Dr. Dang at Mintsing while the latter returned to Peking for a year's study. Dr. Huang had told me of her concern for her nephews and nieces who were being reared in her ancestral home upriver from Shanghai. She came from an old banking and merchant family. The children were exposed to an atmosphere of idleness and indulgence, trained and taught by their servants. They knew little of their mother, who led the life of the idle rich, and almost nothing of their father, who stayed more often than not in Shanghai as a banker. Dr. Huang had now arranged for one of these children to join me as my own. So when I met her boat at Pagoda Anchorage below Foochow, a little girl stood beside her. Dr. Huang had asked if I wanted a girl or boy. I preferred a girl, for I felt that Chinese society did not give girls a square deal.

Seven-year-old Little Thunder still kept tight hold of Aunt Huang's hand as we chugged up the Min River. No smile appeared on her face. Later, Little Thunder told me that her servant had said foreign people boiled children's eyes to make medicine.

On our return to Mintsing a big crowd was waiting under the camphor tree to welcome their new doctor. We plunged into the endless tasks of clinics, ward care, supervision of nurses, and direction of servants. We watched the gradual growth of our modest, two-storied new building, fashioned in an L shape to fit into the corner of the wall. This building was to have electric lights and running water, wards and private rooms, an operating room, and rooms on the first floor for men employees.

When everything else was done, we worked in the garden transplanting strawberry plants, putting in tomato plants, moving the precious English violets, starting vegetable seeds. After the evening meal of rice and vegetables, Dr. Dang, Dr. Huang, and I sat in our living room and studied medicine.

9
Fun and Adventures

NOT ALL of our evenings were devoted to serious study, however. Our staff needed to learn how to play too, so I asked them to plan a party. Their program consisted of two hymns, two prayers, and some Bible study. Having survived that "party," I asked if we three doctors might plan the next program. When the nurses and the village preacher came for the second evening of fun, we began by performing skits. They loved it. Then everyone made a speech, the nurses in Foochow dialect, Dr. Huang and the preacher in Mandarin. I too gave a very simple talk in English since they were all anxious to hear this language. Then we played musical chairs. Everyone laughed until their faces ached.

Next we set three lighted candles in a row on the floor. "Look very carefully," we warned. "We will ask someone to walk over them blindfolded." Then we blindfolded Handy Andy, silently blew out the candles in front of him, and writhed with laughter as he walked across the room stepping higher than a proud rooster. Following this performance we played a Chinese game. A line from a famous classic would be quoted to see who could match it with the next line. My teacher offered a line from something I had just studied, so even I was able to match one. Then we played other Chinese memory games, and decided that women were better at deduction and observation, while men were better at concentration. Everyone loved this new kind of party, so we had one every week.

Then we found a small piece of land on which to play badminton.

The Chinese loved this game. Not only our staff, but the village teachers and a preacher or two would appear late every afternoon to join in. October and November passed swiftly with this balance of work and play. Stephen had returned from Shanghai, wired the men's hospital, and set up the Delco plant. Now we had electric lights all over the compound.

December 1925, brought severe cold. Dressed in Chinese padded gowns and wearing padded cloth shoes, we spent cold evenings in our parlor studying medicine. The party evenings were warm enough without a fire because we were all so active with games and laughter, but on ordinary evenings as I watched the thermometer in the parlor go down to 54, 50, and even 48 degrees before bedtime, I never really came to accept it. Though their older people and some women carried a fire basket around during the coldest days, the people of Mintsing had no fireplaces and were thus accustomed to a cold that even a hardy New Englander found hard to live with.

All through the cold winter months Dr. Huang and I took turns riding various circuits to hold clinics. One circuit led us through Fifth, Ninth, Eighth, and Tenth Towns. Another was to Eleventh and Twelfth Towns on the other side of the mountain. Another brought us to Fourteenth and Fifteenth Towns, where we held clinics at Cliff Face, Mountain Peace, and Wind Head. I made the biggest circuit of all when I crossed the River Min to visit the villages along the river, and to the valley beyond Horse Cry Mountain. The Min was wider here than the Connecticut River at Northampton, and I did not know whether a pony could swim so far. Stephen and I decided to load Patter into a small ferryboat, but we worried that he might act up and upset us in the middle of the river. Then I remembered reading a book on managing horses when I was young and recalled a method suggested for such an occasion. I took a rope and twisted it under Patter's tail, brought the ends forward between his ears, and got into the boat to pull. Stephen pushed from the rear and Patter entered the boat gracefully. He never moved a muscle all the way across the river. We crossed the river at Little Leaf and followed the river up to Big Leaf, then on to Creek Bottom where we had a

Bearers Above the Min River

church in an old dilapidated house. Hordes of people came to see us, and we treated over a hundred. As the sun began to set we closed our medicine and bedding baskets and started up Horse Cry Mountain, following the Chinese pastor who was taking us to his home for the night. It was a steep climb, up and up old stone stairs, but commanding a wonderful view of the Min River in the deep valley below. At the top we entered a bamboo grove.

"We must proceed with care," announced our host. "Wild boar abound in these groves." Finally we arrived at his little old house. He gave me a room at the top of a ladder, while he and Stephen occupied a second room beyond mine. I was exhausted and went right to sleep, while below the ladder in the candle-lit kitchen, numerous neighbors chatted with the two men and craned their necks to get a glimpse of that strange-looking woman doctor. In the morning we cared for the numerous sick who had arrived from unseen homes in the great bamboo grove. One of them had to be anesthetized for a minor operation on his hand. Stephen put him to sleep on a door laid across sawhorses in the courtyard, while forty or fifty astounded and frightened people looked on. All were greatly relieved when the man woke up a short while later.

Then we continued down into the deep valley of a tributary which joined the Min River at Creek Bottom. I was sure there had to be a path along the river which we could have followed instead of making such a spectacular climb. The pastor who guided us perhaps had his reasons, however, and I was young and strong and loved new adventures. The mountains were loftier on the southern side of the Min, and the people more backward. There were few schools for boys and none for girls, most of whom still had bound feet. We passed very beautiful waterfalls which spilled over dramatic cliffs before at last arriving at Upper Plateau. Here we spent the night in another ancient house. As usual, the men gathered to talk with Stephen, the women with me. Most of the conversation concerned bandits and their cruel raids, the terrible poverty and illnesses; we heard a meticulous recital of the prices of rice, cloth, chicken, pork, and other commonly used commodities. We listened also to stories of spirits and ghosts. We were told what they had paid for the child-wives of their sons.

The next morning the basket carriers were conversing beneath my window when I awoke. "Today we cross Horse Cry Mountain at its highest point," one of them said.

"Yes, and will this horse cry!" answered another.

"No horse has ever gone over this mountain in ten thousand years," added the first.

Others came to squat with them and to conjecture how much Patter would weep during the coming climb. After a breakfast of wet rice and salted vegetable, we started to climb Horse Cry. The steep stone stairs led straight up, and I counted them by stopping for a rest at the end of every hundred steps. In all there were twelve hundred stone stairs, each worn in the middle by centuries of passing feet; in addition there was much steep earthen path. It took four hours to get to the top, but Patter disappointed the bearers and did not cry. We looked down over a striking panorama, with the Min Valley ahead of us and the mountains of Mintsing beyond.

On our way down we stopped at any little hamlet where sick people wanted treatment, and it took several more hours to come to Little Leaf on the edge of the River Min. From this place we would take the upriver launch to Water Mouth. While we waited for the boat, we saw a little boy industriously plying a ferry-boat back and forth across a small stream that flowed into the Min River. He was singing something to the tune of a beautiful old Chinese melody, and at last I caught the words:

The foreign woman sits under a tree,
Knitting industriously;
The foreign woman sits under a tree
Working busily.

Finally the launch arrived. We scrambled aboard to enjoy the cool trip upriver to Water Mouth, a huddle of houses on the river bank, their foundations supported by long poles set into the bank. A street ran on the other side of this row of houses, parallel to the river, and another row of houses could be seen on its opposite side. Our host was a young Mr. Sia, who made his living selling medicines and prescribing for the townspeople. This town, too, had no real doctor. We spent a pleasant evening and night in his clean home, visiting back and forth with the local military authorities. We talked about gardens, horses, and bandits.

Sometime later, back in Mintsing again, a stranger appeared at the hospital asking for a doctor to go through bandit-infested country to a village where a woman lay injured, shot in a bandit raid the previous night. Two of the bandits had been captured by the local soldiers, and the men on our staff as well as our neighbors had all run over to the military headquarters to see them tortured into confession. Only our old helper, Handy Andy, remained at home to give advice on whether or not to visit the village. "Bandits are lurking in the woods around the village," he said. "I dare not give my consent for you to go. But I will write to the yamen for advice." *

The official in the yamen finally sent back word that he was ordering ten soldiers to accompany me on this medical expedition. I thought that it might be even more dangerous to enter bandit territory with ten soldiers armed to the teeth; nevertheless, I graciously accepted the gallant escort and jumped on Patter. With a mad snort the horse galloped out the front gate and along the path upriver. Stephen was just returning from the yamen, looking sick from the tortures he had witnessed. I looked back to see him seize an umbrella from an astonished pedestrian and whirl around to start after me. Patter rushed along the narrow path toward Third Town following the man who had come for me. Stephen was hurrying along some distance behind. Strung out behind him came the ten soldiers, chugging along single file and none too happy about their assignment. Women stood at the gateways of their homes exclaiming, "There goes the doctor! What is she doing, rushing off in that di-

* A yamen was the headquarters and residence of an official.

rection as the sun descends?" Another yelled, "Ten soldiers are following her. Surely she must be going to that dangerous place."

We went down stone stairs and came to a creek with a horse tooth bridge. I skipped behind our guide across the tall stone teeth which sat in a row across the stream, with Stephen close behind and Patter splashing through the water. Now we were in a very narrow valley with fragrant pines, steep hills rising abruptly on either side. My host pointed silently toward smoke rising from the trees above us on the right, and I knew what he meant. We walked very silently from there on. Eventually we came to a rough wooden bridge and crossed over to the bandit side. Finally we came to a small group of deserted houses which surrounded a fort-like structure. It was perfectly silent; not a person appeared.

The guide led Stephen and me into the fort. It was completely dark and my heart stood still. Perhaps this was a bandit leading me into captivity. I was glad Stephen had come. We climbed a ladder, still in complete darkness. Above I heard the clank of guns. Finally someone lit a little red candle, and I saw that the room was packed with armed men. These were the village men. Their women and children had been sent off to safety in some other village.

A groan came from the furthest corner. We crossed quickly to find a woman in great pain, her shoulder shattered. We dressed the wound, gave her something for pain, and urged the silent men to send her to our hospital.

When we emerged from the fort it was already dark, and the silent string of ten soldiers was just arriving. I told them we were now ready to return. "Too dangerous, too dangerous," replied the corporal. "We will have to spend the night here." But I was certain we did not want to spend the night in that packed room with standing room only. It was now raining and very cold.

Then two village men offered to take us back. "The hills are full of bandits," one of them whispered. "We will go without any sound."

I felt colder than ever. One man led, and I followed close enough to listen to his footsteps. Behind me came Patter. Going down some stone stairs, Patter stumbled and fell with an awful clatter. We were all paralyzed with fear, but nothing happened and we went on through the cold, rainy black night.

As we passed a house which lurked in the shadows, a man stepped out silently and handed us an umbrella. Further on, our guides stopped at another house and emerged with a paper lantern and candle. "It is all right to light it now," one of them said. With the tiny flicker from the candle we traveled the narrow path above a rocky, dashing stream until at last we came to the horse tooth bridge. Apparently families all along the way were watching our progress and helping out—but it was rather spooky.

The next day I was called again to see the woman and found her in shock. I bundled her into a long chair, had men fasten carrying poles to it, and then sent them off to the hospital on the run. I chose another path so we would not hinder each other. Patter and I galloped along one trail while the four men dashed along a path just across the stream from me. With proper treatment at the hospital the woman rallied quickly, and in time she made a full recovery.

And so our days passed by with more or less exciting and challenging events as we traveled over the country vaccinating, delivering babies, and preaching the gospel of better health and child care.

10

Farewell to Stephen and Dr. Huang

SUMMER 1926, CAME around and it was time for Stephen to go to Nanking for the agriculture course that he longed to take. Not only did he love to grow things, but he also possessed a tremendous urge to help the farmers improve their techniques and thus attain a higher level of production and livelihood. His whole heart was in this, and I was thrilled that our hospital could serve this worthy project by sending Stephen to study modern agriculture.

Though it was hard to see Stephen go, we knew he would return to continue working with us in Mintsing. With Dr. Huang it was different. In October, this dedicated Chinese woman doctor departed for Central China. We stood under the old camphor tree, heartbroken, as we saw her off. Dr. Huang was loved by all the people in and around the hospital. She was highly intelligent and capable, and she had learned the Foochow language very quickly. She took great interest in each patient; she was well-acquainted with Chinese thinking and customs and treated them with great respect. At the same time she was modern and eagerly helped me make improvements.

We now had a hundred beds for patients and each bed was always occupied. Our reputation had grown immensely and I had been seriously considering asking for the medical work at the county seat. Dr. Dang had returned from her year of study in Peking, and we were prepared to make an even more substantial contribution to our county. Now we had a real sterilizer, our new hospital for men was painted, and a carpenter was busy making screens for every window in the compound. A graduate from our Foochow hospital had come to direct the nursing school and to prepare our students for the national examinations.

Because we were making such rapid progress, and because the need was so great, I had pleaded with the missionary committee in Foochow to allow Dr. Huang to stay. I told them of our progress and our plans for the future.

"You built that new hospital building," they pointed out. "That took money. We just cannot add her salary to our present budget."

I pointed out that the money for the hospital came from a gift given to Dr. Carleton many years before and that the Board had given permission for the construction. Local money was not used for it. But they would not listen. They would not approve the extra expense, and that was final. Not one medical person stood on the committee. To the committee, evangelism was more important than medicine. These people were ill-equipped mentally to recognize the value of our medical work. Perhaps it was more than that. Very likely they all knew that I had not proved to be a "hot-hearted" evangelist, and for that reason they probably felt the funds should go elsewhere.

I had returned discouraged to Mintsing and broke the news to Dr. Huang. I asked her if she would be willing to go to the Foochow hospital to work for a year while I sought financial help directly from the Board in the States. It would take time, but I felt that within a year her salary could have been assured. But now I knew instinctively that she would not stop at the Foochow hospital. There she would not have the feeling of equality that she had in Mintsing. I knew she would go back to Central China. We had lost her. Little Thunder, my adopted daughter, started off bravely for school without a tear. But I knew that her heart ached because of the departure of her Aunt Huang.

I was stunned. Not only had a good friend left us, but she was a wonderful doctor that our work could ill afford to lose. What would now come of our plans for future medical services for this country? I felt bitter that my fellow missionaries had done this thing. It was shameful to me that those who claimed to spread the gospel could not see the good done to the Chinese people by this medical work. My dreams had been shattered. But I had to pick up the pieces and carry on day by day.

11

November Vicissitudes

NOVEMBER 1926, CAME with its bare red-brown fields and trees laden with white waxberries. Men busily cut the berries on the mountains and brought them home in baskets for their women to make into candles for the winter. The men were also busy stacking rice straw around poles stuck in the ground; this straw would feed the family buffalo and stuff new mattresses. This was the time for mending broken bamboo baskets and for patching cracks in the mud walls of homes. And when the fields were cleared of rice straw, and after every fallen kernel had been gleaned by driving flocks of geese over the bare earth, the farmers began to put in their winter wheat.

This November brought an evangelist from Foochow who held meetings in the schools, church, and our hospital. Our little chapel was packed with ambulatory patients, staff and servants, and neighbors from the nearby street. The earnest missionary ranted for a good long time and finally announced in firm tones, "Everyone who is going to give up his idols, please stand." There was a pause. Everyone looked around to see what the others were doing. A few stood, looking around anxiously; then a few more, until eventually everyone was on his feet. The missionary then painstakingly took down every name. Next she broke into a violent tirade against idols before concluding with a prayer of thanksgiving for all the souls that had just been saved.

The next day a deaf old lady who had been in the audience asked Dr. Dang and me, "What was that meeting last night?"

Dr. Dang and I expressed surprise. "You stood up," we reminded her. "Do you know what you stood up for? Do you know they wrote your name down?"

"I stood up because everyone stood up," she replied indignantly. "If the Foreign Born asks us to stand, we stand."

I thought then that it is not just the "heathen" who have idols. Almost everyone has a paltry little god that he sets up on a pedestal and worships. Many of us worship power or prestige or possessions or pleasure. The idols we worship are more pernicious and perverting than the "heathen's" because we do not realize the nature of our adoration and are unaware that such worship destroys our character. What would the good missionaries do to me if they knew my thoughts? Well, I would never utter them, for I had found a place to give myself in service. I would take no risks of being sent home as a heretic. Perhaps I was not honest with the missionaries. But I was now seeing that the most important thing was to be honest with myself.

One day we heard the clanging of cymbals and the blare of brass.

We rushed out the front gate to see what was happening. All the people in the street, all our servants, all our staff, and even the ambulatory patients customarily ran to see any unusual event in our neighborhood. A procession was approaching; a large group of men carried a huge paper ship bedecked in green and red characters that gave the name of a dead man. A long line of men and children trailed behind in white garments, while women attired in white or gray, with great straw things on their heads, stumped along at the rear on their bound feet.

The group assembled at the end of the bridge where the ship was launched in our stream as it was set afire. While it drifted slowly away they sent firecrackers booming after it. The ship blazed furiously as it gathered speed in the current. And thus the soul of a departed man was carried across the spiritual river that must be spanned after death. Since this man had died away from home, his spirit had been prevented from crossing. When the little paper craft had burned its last, everyone slowly made his way home over the narrow, stony path, with the women still in the rear.

It was not long after this that we witnessed another riverbank ceremony. This was for another man who had died away from home. His family had to ascertain whether his spirit had accompanied him when his coffin was brought home. The people gathered at the river just as the moon rose, and a row of women began mourning at the top of their voices. At the water's edge a priest danced on a straw mat to the tune of a weird fife. At one end of the mat someone held a long bamboo branch upright; a cock sat proudly at the top of the branch. This ceremony of dance and fife was supposed to continue until the cock crowed, for that was the signal that the spirit had returned safely home. The priest leaped back and forth with bent head, flourishing a long spear, while the fife shrieked on and on. Sometimes the priest turned a somersault or got down on his knees to pray to the dignified rooster perched above him. The whole family, in white, stood in the moonlight in spellbound silence waiting for the cock to crow. But he would not. One of the boy nurses told me that they had given the cock some wine to loosen his tongue. Dusk settled rapidly around us. They poked the cock with a stick. He still would not crow. Finally the head of the family paid the priest and called off the party. The spirit had not crossed over. They would have to consult a fortune teller to find a more auspicious day.

Fragrant Sister's grandfather, a highly respected old gentleman, died later that month of November. Because the family was Christian, and because they had three daughters on our nursing staff, we were all invited. Before attending the funeral we sent our gift, a long piece of good cotton cloth. Attached to this length of cloth were quotations from the Confucian classics in characters cut out of gilt paper which attested to the virtues of the deceased. Each such gift was fastened to a bamboo pole and provided a banner for the funeral procession.

When we arrived at the family home, the whole family sat on the earthen floor around the body, wailing according to custom. At the head of the old grandfather sat the two sons, dressed in sackcloth and wearing sackcloth caps with two ears. Next in order sat the grandsons, also in sackcloth but with yellow caps. Then came the daughters-in-law and female children of the sons, all of whom wore yellow caps. The daughters and their children sat near the grandfather's feet, and they were wearing white caps with ears. The old grandmother sat on the ground at her husband's feet crying and wailing louder than all the rest. The children, frightened no doubt, wailed and shrieked.

When Pastor Ding arrived and began the Christian service, the family sat in silence. Little Grandmother fell fast asleep on the ground. Then hymns were sung, and a great black coffin was brought in. The mourners broke into deafening wails. Grandmother woke up and tried to throw herself into the coffin with Grandfather, but her sons restrained her and some of the women took her out of the room. Quicklime having been placed in the bottom, the men gently laid the body in the coffin. They covered the body with long reeds before the heavy cover was nailed down.

Then a feast began for hundreds of guests. Beggars for miles around arrived and wandered between the tables looking for leftovers.

Finally, the coffin was carried in an impressive procession from the home, through the village and across the bridge. Slowly the procession made its way over the narrow path to the hills below Ko Iong. Led by a band of drums, cornets, and flutes, and with colorful banners unfurled, the funeral procession at last reached the red soil of the grave.

In contrast, the next memorable event was a happy occasion. Second Little Sister, one of the nurses, was to be married. Her parents had made the engagement, with the help of a fortune teller and a go-between, when she was a small child. The couple had never met. We were invited to the Day-Before Feast at her home. The bride's friends and relatives would not be invited to the wedding feast at her husband's home; that celebration was reserved for the bridegroom's relatives and friends only. When Dr. Dang and I arrived, the courtyard was already full of women and children; the men stood outside chatting. The mother led us to Second Little Sister's bedroom where we found her on the bed crying bitterly.

"Does she feel so badly about being married?" I asked.

"Oh, it is not that. She must cry to show that she is filial and does not want to leave home. She does not cry all the time. She just cries when anyone comes to see her," Dr. Dang explained.

We approached the bed and spoke to her, but she kept her face covered, said not a word and continued to cry with a passion. Women standing nearby nodded approvingly and commented on the propriety of her grief.

Finally we sat down to a feast for about a hundred guests. Eight people sat on benches at each bare wooden table, and each guest had a bowl and a pair of chopsticks. A big bowl of hot food appeared in the middle of the table, and we all dipped in our chopsticks, bringing out food by the mouthful. That bowl nearly finished, another appeared. And so it went through perhaps twenty dishes, each interspersed with much talking and gaiety, in the course of the next two hours. There were bowls of pork and chicken and several dishes of seafood, including shark's fins, shrimp, a small black fish, intestines from a large fish, bird's nest soup, and a large fish cooked—head and all—in a delicious sweet and sour sauce. Vegetables were cooked in tasty meat soups. Another memorable dish was bean curd in chicken soup. Chickens and dogs wandered under our tables, ready to catch any scrap that might fall. Beggar women wandered in and out also looking for anything we might discard.

Men sent from the bridegroom's home then came to take the bride's belongings to her new home so they would be ready when she arrived the next day. They carried out four beautifully lacquered red dressers as well as boxes of clothes, also in red lacquer with black trimming and gold characters. For her kitchen there were tubs and buckets. The most interesting of these was a red lacquered wooden tub in which she would deliver her babies. In China, women delivered in a squatting position over such a tub into which the newborn child would fall.

On the way home I walked alone thinking about the renewal of life celebrated in this Chinese ceremony. I crossed the long, precarious bridge and followed a winding path through paddy fields to the base of Ko Iong. Out of a recent rain had been born many waterfalls that came crashing down over precipices of blue-gray and red. I climbed past picturesque black rocks, their weather-beaten faces looking out calmly over the green valley and its silvery creek that wound in and out through the bare, red paddy fields. I looked eastward across the river, beyond the hospital to the farther mountains past Third and Fourth Towns. They were partly shrouded by driving rain. Yet, sunlight penetrated four small gray clouds which floated down the valley, transforming them into blazing tongues of fire. It was unusual and astonishingly beautiful. I was struck by the analogy between this scene before me and the way of life. Though we might find ourselves in a raging storm, beyond it there was sunlight and beauty and hope. Though the conditions of man might give rise to despair, in the children there was hope and beauty. I went home filled with great happiness.

12

Farewell to Mintsing

In those years when China was controlled by warlords, we paid hardly any attention to politics and little realized we were soon to witness a revolution. For us in the back country of Fukien, life seemed to go on pretty much as usual, despite the gathering of political forces elsewhere. For example, in December 1926, a fifteen-year-old girl was brought into the hospital by her mother-in-law. She was a northern child, sold by her parents during a famine. She had been brought south to Mintsing where three months earlier she had been married to the son of her purchaser. Her new husband loved her very much, but it was tradition for sons never to interfere in the relationship between mother and bride. Unfortunately, his mother hated the young girl. When we examined the girl we found that her back was raw with whiplashes, her neck had been burned with a red hot iron, and one hip had been beaten with stones into a discolored mass. We found deep knife wounds here and there on her body, and her breasts had been twisted and pinched until they were black. She had not been allowed food or drink for a number of days and was in a state of shock. The local police would do nothing.

Early in January 1927, Pastor Hsu, who was now my teacher in his free time, went to his home in Eleventh Town on some business. I had suspected for some time that he was connected with a growing bandit band there. Even after several days he did not return from his "business"; we began to worry. One night two men arrived from Eleventh Town to see me. "Hsu Sie-ming is desperately ill and his family fears he will not live until morning," they told me. I hesitated. There was that bandit connection, and this was night. Moreover I had a badly sprained ankle which made mounting and dismounting a painful business. On the other hand, Hsu was a man who needed care. Also, I was his pupil; in China that alone would be sufficient reason for my going.

A boy nurse and I started out on the fifteen-mile trip over a bad path lit only by the kerosene lantern carried by our guide. We went over bridge after bridge without railings; one consisted of just a single plank. At midnight we arrived at the Hsu ancestral home. According to custom one was supposed to stand outside the gate until invited in by the family. No one came out, so I continued to stand with the boy nurse. Our guide took care of the horses and then led us in. As we entered the dimly lit room we found Mr. Hsu semiconscious, his whole family crying. His old father refused to speak to me, for he believed only in the old Chinese doctors and had not wanted me to come. My guides had invited me on their own responsibility.

Mr. Hsu had lost much weight and was very weak. He had an enlarged spleen and constantly coughed blood. Attacks of pain were frequent, and I thought of breakbone fever.* Moreover, he had not slept for days; the women of the family would not permit him to sleep for fear he would never wake up. Because this was such a malaria infested area, I guessed this to be the most likely affliction and administered quinine intravenously. Then I gave him something to make him sleep in spite of all the women. Next I said that we had all better get some rest to be strong for the next day. This astonished them, but they agreed. The next morning the family was radiantly happy, for Mr. Hsu had taken a turn for the better. Even the old father was very nice to me and asked me to examine and prescribe for him. Mr. Hsu, who was now fully conscious, smiled at me and said, "This will make you famous."

The next day, Sunday morning, I rode into Sixth Town as the church bells were ringing. Strangely enough, student boys and girls from Foochow were traveling along the upriver paths on their way home from school.

"What has happened?" I asked some of them.

"Schools, churches, and hospitals are all closed," they said. And

* An infectious disease of the tropics and subtropics; it is transmitted by mosquitoes and is characterized by fever, rash, and great pain in the joints.

that was all they would say. I arrived at the hospital with an uneasy feeling, not knowing what was happening in the rest of China.

Once again I was called to see Mr. Hsu and this time found him unconscious. I was sure the family had given him some native drug. To be sure, he had not taken his quinine. "That is a cold medicine," the family yelled at me. "He has a cold disease and must have hot medicine." I gave him another intravenous injection of quinine and waited for him to recover. When it came time to leave, Mr. Hsu looked very sad. The family said he was desperately worried for the hospital. But no one would say why. I had to leave mystified, but considerably saddened by his troubled face. On the way home I wondered, and at last thought it might have some connection with the disturbing conditions in Foochow. Did he get some advance news through his bandit connections?

Entering the hospital gate I was greeted by unsmiling faces. "What is wrong?" I asked Dr. Dang. She led me into the garden and told me that a group of men was coming from the county seat to smash up the hospital and remove the foreign doctor. Mr. Hsu apparently had known but could not tell me in front of the crowd around him.

Gold Sister came running into the garden. "Doctor must not be seen outside our compound," she said anxiously.

Pastor Sia hurried in with a blanched face. "Go off and hide somewhere," he said urgently in a low voice.

"If there is such danger," I replied, "each girl nurse should go home immediately to her own family." But not a girl would go.

However, Moon Blossom, wife of the new cook, came up to me. "I want to take my most precious possession home and then will return at once," she said. A moment later she went lumbering out the front gate like a buffalo trying to run, her baby on her back and a thermos bottle in her hands. Soon she returned with the baby, having hidden the thermos in her nearby home. Dr. Dang and I laughed until we ached.

Just then a telegram arrived from the American consul in Foochow, but it was in code, and what did I know about his codes? Then the two missionary ladies, Edna and Ursula, hurried in wearing very long faces. They were dressed for travel: hats, gloves, coats, umbrellas. "Where in the world are you going?" I asked in great astonishment.

"We were up all night packing things," Edna said indignantly, "and now we are ready to leave Mintsing."

"I have just received a telegram from the consul," I said, holding it upside down. "And as I decipher it, it says, 'All is well. Fear not. Continue your good work.'" The two serious missionary ladies were not helped by my levity.

At four o'clock the next morning there was a great pounding at the gate; it was a messenger from the county seat. We opened the gate and let him in. Only something very serious would bring a man from the county seat in the night. He brought a letter from Mr. Eyestone at the county seat, who wrote in a very serious tone and urged us, "for God's sake," to leave at once. Did he have more recent word than the local officials who had assured us that all was well? How could I know? But I decided to go. Silently we packed our things. Then we were off down the stream.

When we reached the county seat a strange man approached quietly and said, "Would Doctor and her friends go over to the yamen right away?"

We went at once and without fear, for the head of the yamen was the husband of one of the nurses at our hospital. When we arrived, this nurse pulled me into a corner and whispered, "The communist soldiers are coming tonight. You cannot sleep in a boat. You must stay right here."

The general and his nurse wife personally set up beds for all of us and made us welcome. Two soldiers with guns were stationed outside our door. The next morning our host told us that boat after boat packed with communist soldiers had gone upriver during the night on their way from Canton to Nanking. "Now you may go on to Foochow," said the general. "The way should be safe."

We knew that Chiang Kai-shek was on his way north, and that the communists were a part of his army, but we did not understand the political situation and its implications for the future. If Chiang took control of the whole country, and if the communists were given much influence, we feared that anything might happen to foreigners. In Foochow the American consul ordered us out of the city at once. He said that no one could foretell what might happen and that we must go. We had a choice of going north to Shanghai or south to Manila. I could not take Little Thunder out of the country without a long siege of red tape. If I took her to Shanghai, she would go to her old home and I would look for a hospital somewhere. But the consul said that if we went to Shanghai we might be sent home, so it seemed better to go to Manila to wait out the formation of a new order in China. Sadly I watched Little Thunder sail away on the Shanghai steamer with Ursula, one of the missionary ladies who planned to go from there to the United States. Then I went to Manila.

13

Return to China—1928

IT WAS NOW December 1928, and I was aboard an old steamer heading from Shanghai to Foochow. I had just returned to China from a furlough in the United States. I thought of my first trip in 1924, when the nurses from Magaw Hospital had met me with an old houseboat. And then I remembered how I had said a sad farewell to Little Thunder early in 1927 when I had put her on this same ship to Shanghai for her return to Dr. Huang, her aunt. At the time I went to Manila I had suffered a long time with amoebic and bacillary dysentery, as well as a giardia infection.* No one in Manila had great success treating me, so I decided to return to the United States where I was cured in three months. It was

* Giardia, a genus of zooflagellates, inhabits the intestines of mammals; one species is associated with diarrhea in man.

thrilling to feel well again; to swim, play tennis, and plunge into post-graduate work.

Also, it had been most interesting to compare my country with China. I marveled at the spirit of progress and efficiency, the modern knowledge and techniques, the humming speed of American civilization. At the same time I remembered China with her long history of philosophy and high ethical teachings, her love of beauty in nature, in literature, in music and all arts. I thought of China's young people with their great artistic ability, their high intelligence, their reverence for learning, their respect for the aged, and their passionate patriotism. I remembered Chinese ways of courtesy and gentleness; their fine sensitivity and intuition were characteristics in even the illiterate mountain people. Even the poorest people possessed a wonderful graciousness and dignity. Confucius and sons had given their people a great deal.

We Westerners, despite our technology, suffered by comparison. This was demonstrated anew on the ship I now rode. Thirty missionary children were returning to the south for the holidays from their school in Shanghai. The boys and girls screamed in raucous voices. They tore wildly over the decks, knocking against Chinese people without apology. They fell over each other in a way most repugnant to Chinese. They screamed loudly in front of English-speaking Chinese of their anger and revulsion that one of their group had to share a cabin with a Chinese boy. I was ashamed.

Mary Carleton and Stephen Lau waited for me on a launch as we docked downriver from Foochow. It was so good to see them again. They told me that the hospital in Mintsing had been invaded by bandits who had run off with the ponies and left Dr. Dang in a badly shocked state of mind. I was now dreadfully anxious to head upriver to Mintsing as soon as possible.

Events conspired to keep me in Foochow for a few days, however. Customs had seized my cases of medicines, valued at more than $1,000, and a 50 percent customs charge was demanded. At last I found an Englishman who headed the department, and he let me take my cases of medicine away with no charge. Then it was necessary to go to Inland Customs to secure a permit to take my things upriver without paying an additional tax. This time I met a delightful Chinese gentleman, wearing a lovely blue silk robe, who gladly gave me the permit. "All China's improvement is due to the missionary's effort," he said. Then he told me of the government's plans to improve China and of the provincial road-building program. He showed maps of the projected highways, and it was thrilling to see what lay ahead.

My next duty was to call on the bishop and others to secure support to buy a pony that would replace those stolen by the bandits, for I hoped to continue the traveling clinic in Mintsing. Stephen went alone to look over various animals being offered for sale; prices would have risen if a foreigner were seen. After the prices were fixed he took me to see two or three, and we chose a young, gentle white mare, six months in foal, with good feet and wind.

During those days in Foochow I learned something of the new regime headed by Chiang Kai-shek. Chiang's government had instituted many reforms and new laws. For example, women were now legally equal to men. They had the right of inheritance, the right to choose their own husbands, and even the right to divorce. A man was now allowed only one wife at a time. This was so different from the conditions in China when I left in 1927. Furthermore, the new government had notified all Taoist monks, as well as those who made "idol paper" and incense sticks, to find new jobs within three months. Cartloads of idols had been taken out of the Foochow temples and burned in great bonfires. Temples had been occupied by the government and no longer served as places of worship. Clean-up days were set, and even city officials could be seen out sweeping the streets with brooms. College girls campaigned against the display of uncovered fruit in the street shops. It seemed as though a new spirit had come to the city.

I learned that Stephen was now teaching at the Boys' School at the county seat in Mintsing. In addition to teaching he raised vegetables, fruit, and flowers; he also conducted agricultural experiments. At the completion of his year at the Agricultural School in Nanking, he had brought back four thoroughbred baby female goats which he raised. He gave flower seeds to each pastor and encouraged each to beautify his grounds. He gathered the farmers for institutes in which he delivered lectures on ways to improve their crops. He had also interested General Bing Hu, commander of the troops in Mintsing, in this work. Bing Hu and his officials were now contributing money to aid these projects for the improvement of the county.

At last, just before Christmas, we had finished all business in Foochow. Trunks, suitcases, groceries, one pony, three boatmen, twenty-six cases of medicines, Stephen, and I packed on board a five-bed river boat for the trip inland. It was so bitterly cold that I suspect none of us slept; we just kept our eyes shut and waited for dawn. When the first gray light finally crept over the mountains, I watched in pure delight as the warm gold moved down to the low green hills which rose from either side of the clear Min River.

Stephen came to sit with me and tell me of his experiences when the soldiers in the Northern Campaign arrived in Nanking. "Dr. Williams was killed by them?" I asked.

"Yes, they shot him. As he lay on the ground the nurses ran out and knelt around him. The soldiers pointed their guns at the girls, but boy students formed a ring around them and saved them."

I remembered meeting Dr. C. S. Trimmer who had been there at the time. Trimmer said that when he realized what was happening, he quickly painted his face with Mercurochrome and came out acting insane. In this way he thought he had saved his life, for Chinese apparently would not harm the insane.

My thoughts came back to Stephen who sat there so quietly. "What did you do?" I asked.

"Dr. Martin had a valuable herd of sixty thoroughbred cows. Another student helped me herd them out of the city to safety."

"Were any other missionaries hurt?" I knew about them, but wanted to see how much he would tell. Not much, I discovered.

"I gave my coat to a young missionary man who was running away and he escaped in that disguise. Many boy students stripped off their coats to cover missionaries in this fashion." He paused for a moment. "Many people, farmers and women, some of them very poor, gave all their money to buy the lives of missionaries. Some of the women took off their hair ornaments and their rings to buy lives."

In spite of the turmoil, Stephen had loved the year of study in Nanking, and his conversation constantly reverted to goats, rabbits, sheep, dogs, fruit trees, vegetables and soil, as well as ideas of what could be done to help Mintsing farmers.

People were waiting to greet us when we arrived at the hospital in Mintsing. Dr. Dang looked very ill. I knew she needed a vacation right away, but she decided to stay until I had settled in to the work. The whole atmosphere of the hospital was tense. Bandits had threatened to return, and people now knew our hospital was not inviolable. The place was nearly empty.

A few nights later Dr. Dang and I stood on the veranda looking out into the darkness. We had been alerted by the barking of our neighbors' dogs. Boats could be seen moving swiftly upstream, and across the creek someone was running fast upriver with a lighted lantern. This was most unusual for that quiet town. Then we saw a bright, glaring light downstream in a little village; it died down and came up again three times. This signal was answered in like manner from the roof of a shop right on our street. Soon the same signal was seen far upstream, and we realized that bandit movements were being reported from village to village. The next day a messenger came from the yamen at the county seat carrying a letter which told me never to see an unknown visitor until a responsible person had first interviewed him. The letter also warned that our gatewoman must be very careful, for the yamen had learned that some bandits wanted to take me for ransom.

Some days later we awoke to see black smoke rolling high into the sky from Fifteenth Town, a few miles downriver. We learned that 600 bandits had surrounded and attacked the beautiful new house of an official whom we had been treating. Although it was strongly fortified, the bandits had succeeded in setting it on fire. Then they shot at anyone who tried to escape the flames. One little son was shot in the knee, but managed to crawl out of sight. Later his neighbors brought him to us, but the bandits had seized the little boy's mother and father. Their chests were slit open with knives before they were burned to death tied to stakes. Because of this, 300 marines from Foochow rushed up to do battle with the bandits in Fifteenth Town. We could hear the firing as we stood under the camphor tree looking downstream. People from Fifteenth Town could be seen running up both sides of the river toward us, panting and sweating as they ran to hide in the woods. One of our missionary women, very red of face, came hurrying by. I called to her to stop and have a cup of tea, but she was not amused. I wandered into the room of the little old lady who worked for us whom we called Church Aunt. I found her and the whole staff down on their knees praying for our safety.

The new male nurse, Cung Dai, and the new District Superintendent, Sia, were waiting to talk with me privately. "The bandits may be here before daylight," Mr. Sia said very gravely.

"What should I do?" I asked.

"You two doctors must slip out after dark and go to Eighteenth Fair to sleep," he said firmly.

"I agree with you that Dr. Dang should go, since she cannot stand much more," I answered.

"No," said Cung Dai, "you must both go."

"But I have had no quarrel with them. Why should I go?" I demanded.

"Because," said Mr. Sia with a very white and grave face. "They might take you to be their *t'ai-t'ai*."

Goose pimples came out all over me when I heard the word for wife, and I said meekly, "I will first send home all the girl nurses and then we two doctors will go." But later Dr. Dang and I stepped softly out through the rear gate, thinking the front might be watched, walked through the dark to the Girls' School and slept there.

No bandits came to Sixth Town, however. Near the end of January 1929, 600 soldiers arrived at the county seat from Foochow. The bandits then retreated to Eleventh Town. This was an opportunity for Dr. Dang to get to the county seat safely, and from there to Foochow for her much-needed rest. We told no one that she was going. A chair suddenly appeared, she got into it and was off. Mr. Sia personally escorted her all the way to the county seat.

One day some time later Mr. Sia and I crossed the shaky bridge and headed downstream about a mile. There we could see about fifty bandits running single file on Ko Iong, with fifty or so soldiers and a bugler, also in single file, running after them. The bugler blew vociferously while the bandits and soldiers banged their guns noisily as they climbed. But as the sun began to drop behind Ko Iong, the bugler called the soldiers back for supper; thus the battle ended.

Somewhat later 1,000 soldiers entered Eleventh Town to fight the bandits who were now massed in Twelfth Town. We thought how easy it would be for the bandits to slip up to Ko Iong from that side just as they had from our side of the mountain. Once over the mountain, it would be easy to drop down on Sixth Town and capture it. A girl nurse came running to my house. "They are *really* coming tonight," she said, looking very pale. Someone else came running in. "The bandits are really going to get you because you are just back from America and must have money."

Again I sent all the girls back to their own homes. Then I called Mr. Sia for advice. He told me that every merchant in the street had received a letter from the bandits saying they must give $1,000 each. It was true that the bandits were really expected that night, but 300 soldiers were waiting for them. I was satisfied with that. Later that night Cung Dai came over with a Chinese man's gown and cap. "You just put these on and move quietly out the back gate if anyone comes," he said. I wondered if I could fool anyone. I hung the long gown on my bedpost, set the cap on top, and went to sleep.

Some days later a letter arrived from the American consul in Foochow. He wanted to know what was happening in Sixth Town and ordered me to leave if the soldiers were defeated. I thought that he was the one who ought to know what was happening, and wondered how one could have escaped if the soldiers had been defeated.

14

New Faces, the Coming of Spring, and Questioning

WHILE I HAD been in the United States several new people had joined the hospital staff. One of these was Cung Dai, a bright young preacher from Fourteenth Town. He had been thinking seriously about his life while he prepared his weekly sermons, made visits through his parish, and helped people with their problems. He had been especially fascinated by the story of Jesus washing his disciples' feet. "I thought for a long time about this," he said, "and I asked myself in what way I could give the best service with humility in this community. In the end I thought I could obey the command, 'Even as you do it unto the least of these,' by caring for the sick."

"That is what I, too, have thought all these years," I replied.

"Caring for the sick means helping everyone whether poor or rich, whether a good church member, a dirty beggar, sly thief, or bold bandit," he continued. "At last I decided to leave my pulpit and become a student nurse if the doctors would accept me." This was a young man of unusual intelligence, ability, and sensitivity. I was very pleased to have him join us and hoped that we might find more of his caliber in the future.

Autumn Sister also came from Fourteenth Town. "My husband is an opium addict," she explained sadly. Her husband had had a very responsible government position, but since becoming an opium addict, he could do no work. Autumn Sister wanted to work in the hospital to support her husband and little son. She was a sturdy and sensible young woman who had a good influence on our small staff. Again I was pleased with Dr. Dang's choice.

Another new member was Mrs. Dang, the new "Bible woman" who had come to help Church Aunt. She, like many women in Mintsing, had been sold in infancy to her future parents-in-law. When she was old enough, she had been married to the son of the family. She had had three children. "Then my husband saw another woman he wanted, so he sold me to a man who was very cruel," she told me. She had run away from this man and found her way back to her parents. Fortunately they had taken pity on her and bought her back. Her parents had sent her to school at Eighteenth Fair, and finally she enrolled in our Bible school. There she met teacher Dang, a nice young bachelor who fell in love with her. I could see that this was a happy marriage. We had arranged for Mr. Dang and their pretty little adopted daughter to live in the hospital compound, so the family was kept intact.

"Do you ever see your three children?" I asked.

She shook her head sadly. "Never will it be allowed," she said.

The bitter cold winter of 1928–29 passed, and spring came again. By the middle of March the winter wheat had been harvested and the turnips had been dug. Men were busy ploughing with their great water buffalo. After ploughing, they carried big, open buckets of night soil to fertilize each plot of paddy. One small plot in each area had already been flooded and walled off with mud banks, and the soil was mixed with water until it approached the consistency of cake batter. It was then smoothed off with a long-handled roller before being seeded. These plots were the source of the seedlings which later would be transplanted to the paddies. We could see the blue-clad farmers walking slowly around these small plots as they scattered the yellow rice kernels.

It took thirty days before the rice sprouts were ready for transplanting. During that month the farmers weeded in a most tedious and painstaking manner. Two sawhorses would be set in the plot in such a way that no seedlings were disturbed. Then the farmers would sit on one sawhorse, reaching down to pull all the weeds they could in that position before shifting to the next sawhorse. In this manner they progressed across the plot without disturbing it, collecting all the weeds they pulled in small bamboo baskets fastened to their belts. During that month of waiting they continued to plough and flood the paddy fields. Buffalo manure, carefully saved all through the winter, was burned in small mounds of black earth mixed with rice straw. After being sifted through a bamboo screen, this preparation was added to the paddies.

When it came time to transplant, the farmers pulled up the young rice sprouts, placed them in small bundles, and carried them into the paddies in bamboo baskets. One man would walk ahead with a stick, which he punched into the ooze at regular intervals in curving rows across the field. The planters would follow, taking a few rice shoots at a time, thrusting the roots into a basket of the fertilizer fastened to their belts, and finally setting the seedlings down in the prepared bed. By the end of April, the valley all around was very beautiful; its countless squares, triangles and half circles of luxuriant, tender green rice resembled lovely, soft green carpets stretching as far as the eye could see.

In colorful contrast, the roses bloomed recklessly all through February, March, and April in the little garden we maintained in the compound. By the end of March, the English violets were in full bloom, while the calla and Easter lillies were ready to blossom. The peach blossoms were fading and a fire bush was in full bloom. We trimmed the orange, lemon, lime, and pomelo trees; we planted corn, lettuce and radishes. In April the compound had become intoxicatingly fragrant with the blossoming orange and pomelo trees.

But in the midst of all this beauty we still saw much of the ugliness of reality. The hospital once again was overflowing with patients. Now we had a central kitchen and a woman to do all the cooking, so it was no longer necessary to house the relatives of patients. Many soldiers came to be treated. Some of them told of the capture of the bandit chief who had invaded our hospital and stolen our ponies while I was in

America. The soldiers had run wires through his hands; then they dragged him by these wires along the ground for the nineteen miles to the county seat.

One Sunday morning I awoke to the sound of soft rain on the big banana leaves outside my windows. Suddenly it reminded me of the soft sound of sleet falling on a cold New England day. Homesickness gripped me profoundly. I went to church with Dr. Dang and the nurses, but I was far away. I felt frightfully cut off from home. The people there all seemed like dim figures in a dream. World affairs, fashions, music, new books—all were far away and there was no way I could relate to them. How could I ever go back to the United States after the years of isolation here and find anything in common with others? I sat in the pew looking out the church window at great green pomelo leaves being washed clean in the pouring rain; beyond them rose a range of sublime mountains in soft blue. I began to see that the door was closing behind me; I could no longer stand at the threshold of this beauty. It was necessary to enter. Despite my loneliness, I decided to keep right on with my program of work. And in spite of bandit attacks, we did manage to carry on with our work.

Yet, one evening when I went to Eighteenth Fair to have supper with two American missionary ladies, I was shocked to discover I could not feel the beauty of my surroundings. When I looked at the mountains, tinted lavender by the setting sun, that surrounded the valley; at the foreground with a quaint, thatched mill, its great water wheel set against drooping willows; at the huddle of blue-gray houses sleeping serenely as they had for centuries—it seemed suddenly that a gulf had come between me and all beauty. I could not feel the exquisiteness of the scene.

But after a good American meal and two hours of English conversation, I went prancing home in high spirits. Old U Chai with his lantern could hardly keep up with me. The cool darkness with brilliant stars, the fragrance of the wind, the murmuring river once again seemed to be a part of me. I had a feeling of oneness with all nature. And thus

I saw that, for me, some companionship with those of my own background was indeed necessary, at least for a time.

During this time I continued to question my own values and those of my Christian heritage. I could no longer accept a religion which demanded prayer and faith. Prayer for things or benefits? Faith in what? It was all too shallow and I could not accept the religion of the missionaries around me. More and more I believed that truth and love must be the foundation stones for my beliefs. Still I remained dissatisfied. One could seek truth, but how would one know if it had been found? And how did one find love? I remained baffled, but dared not express my thoughts. I concluded that I was looking for something that was not really attainable.

I turned my back on that mystical, half-perceived world, along with childhood-inculcated ideas of God. I now knew there was no God. I would swim or sink depending on my own efforts and guided by what intellect I had. I had drifted to agnosticism and perhaps very close to the sunless land of atheism.

15
Back on the Track of Modernization, and a New Baby

IN 1929 WE launched forth on the next step of what I had envisioned during my first month at Mintsing in 1924. We asked the staff to think of programs they might put on to show the evils or stupidity of the most common and undesirable customs in the county. The staff was fired with enthusiasm, and everyone spent many hours planning what to do, say, and wear. The first program was aimed at the common people; our chapel was packed full of patients and people from the village. The girls sang cute little songs, set to familiar Chinese tunes, about brushing teeth, swatting flies, and the dangers of eating opium. Then came a skit which showed a nurse who met various people as she traveled on a path. She informed them about scabies, tuberculosis, and other diseases. The ignorant answers given to her questions by those she met provided gales of laughter from the audience. Thus we had them laughing at their own ignorance and superstition. Dr. Dang gave a talk on vitamins and exhibited a brood of rats that had been raised on various diets. That the runt of the lot had been brought up on rice made a tremendous impression on the audience.

Next we invited teachers, scholars, officials, and army officers, who again packed the chapel. Like the first audience, they were highly pleased with the entertainment. Finally the audiences became so large that the programs had to be held on the tennis court; even then the place was packed. This was part of my dream to lift the burden of superstition and ignorance from the people, as well as to heal the sick. Behind the project now was the strong support of the staff, the village people, and the intelligentsia.

One day Cung Dai came to my office. "My uncle has a month-old baby girl that he wants to sell or give away," he said. "Would the doctor like to see this baby?" How did he know that I had decided to take another child? It was common knowledge because I had called in Ho Seing, the sewing woman, who was already busy making up a complete outfit of baby clothes. Everything I did was usually reported far and wide, so naturally he knew. Cung Dai came from an excellent family, with many scholars among his ancestors. The whole family appeared to be intelligent, healthy, and of fine character.

That evening Dr. Dang and I followed Cung Dai past Eighteenth Village to the village of Above-The-Bank. The baby's father was an honest, sincere, and hardworking farmer. The mother was neatly dressed and seemed to be an intelligent woman. They greeted us warmly and gave us cups of hot, fragrant tea—just a few leaves were put in the bottom of the cup or bowl with boiling water poured over them.

"We have a chance to get a month-old baby for my four-year-old son," the mother explained. "It would be just right for me to nurse her." I understood. It would cost $200 to $400 each to obtain a bride for each son, to say nothing of the terrible expense of a wedding. This way the mother could get a month-old baby girl for little or nothing and bring her up to her own ways.

She put her little daughter in my arms. I looked at the plump, sweet little face; the bright, intelligent eyes; the well-developed body with strong energetic movements of legs and arms. I knew this was the baby I had been waiting for. The mother, father, and three intelligent boys stood around me in a half circle, watching me anxiously. I was deciding the future of their beloved little sister. Cung Dai stood in the background, silent and sympathetic. Dr. Dang sat beside me, stroking the baby's head. "This is the one I want," I said. "May I take her home tonight?" The mother looked alarmed.

"I must first make clothes for her," she protested.

If I don't take her now I may never get her, I thought. I was worried that they might decide to give her away as a childwife rather than trust her to the vagaries of an unmarried foreign woman. "I have clothes all made for her," I said smilingly.

"Yes," said Dr. Dang. "She has made all the preparations for a baby."

"Let your heart be at peace. I have everything ready," I said.

"It is getting late. The doctors must go home before dark," urged Cung Dai.

"Yes," agreed the father. "They must not be out late at such a time."

I grasped the baby tightly in my arms and started for the door. The four year old, who had to have a baby bride, began to howl loudly. The mother's face was tight with grief. Neighbor women, who had crowded into the background, laughed heartily at the idea of taking a baby without weeks of negotiating and consultation with a fortune teller.

That night guns boomed out of the darkness around us. Bandits had descended on the town. The great village drum rumbled out its warning. Through the windows we saw spurts of gunfire on all sides. Excited screaming and shouting rose in the street. Gun shots were now coming fast and furious. People outside the wall of the compound were running desperately this way and that. Carrying the squalling baby, I led the nurses and women servants to the secret hiding place that U Chai had made. One by one they crept in. They urged me to join them. "Not with a crying baby," I laughed. Then U Chai and I pulled boxes and baskets into a high pile against the false partition.

I stood in my garden, which was fairly well protected by the buildings from flying bullets, and fed the baby her first bottle. Then I made my way through the dark compound to investigate the situation. I found that Mrs. Dang, the new Bible woman, had disguised herself as an old country woman and had crept into a bed in the ward. I thrust the baby, now wrapped in coarse country clothes, into her arms. If the invaders caught me they would surely kill the baby if they found her in my arms. By midnight it was all over. The bandits did not enter the compound.

By this time my other adopted daughter, Little Thunder, was a studious, sedate girl of twelve. It was time to give her a school name. Since I was, of course, totally unprepared for the task of picking out sister names for the girls, I asked two of the teachers to do this. After many days of consultation, they came with their suggestions. "I hope they are flower names," I said.

"Oh, no, flower names are only for slave girls," Dr. Dang said quickly.

"We suggest 'Hwa' for the common name," began one of the girl teachers.

"Is that the 'Hwa' meaning 'China'?" I asked.

"Yes, it is. Then for the individual names, we thought you might like 'Hui' for Little Thunder; it means 'sunlight,' among other things. And for the baby you might have 'Sing,' which means 'starlight.' "

"China's Sunlight and China's Starlight," I said slowly. "I think I like the thought." And indeed these names seemed appropriate for the girls I had such high hopes for as citizens of the new China.

With the growing danger of bandits in the following months, and the consequent uncertainty of life for anyone in the county, I began to worry about the childrens' future, should something happen to me. I knew that Hwa Hui could go back to her Aunt Huang, but I was particularly worried about Hwa Sing. It seemed to be a good idea to establish a close relationship with her family, not only because of a possible disaster, but also because I thought it would be better for her to know her family. Cung Dai therefore arranged for me and the baby to make a formal call on the grandmother, the oldest member of the family.

This I did according to local custom. I rode in a chair and carried the baby in my lap. Fastened to the chair was a bundle of noodles, the symbol of long life; the noodles were wrapped in red paper, the color of happiness. The package of noodles was a gift for the whole family. Also I took a string of cookies for the boys, as well as some soft cakes for the old grandmother. All along the way people rushed out to see what the "Foreign Devil" was doing riding around with a Chinese baby in her arms.

The family was expecting me at the home in Above-The-Banks village, so a big crowd of women had gathered to watch my every movement and to listen to the strange enunciation of the foreign woman. Everyone in the family had to hold Hwa Sing. All exclaimed, as was polite, how fortunate the baby was. I took Hwa Sing's picture with her old grandmother and hoped that later she might treasure it. This old lady, who was also Cung Dai's grandmother, had seventeen grandsons and eleven granddaughters.

"She is big for her age," someone observed of the baby.

"What does she eat that she is so beautiful?" another asked.

That was my opportunity to tell them what she ate, that she was bathed every day, that she had cod liver oil and orange juice every day. I had a chance to tell them a little about vitamins, and why they were needed to build a good healthy body. This was all new to them—feeding a baby cow's milk in a bottle! There, if a mother had no milk, some other woman in the big family would nurse it. If worse came to worst, a mother would chew up rice and spit it into the baby's mouth.

No one had baby bottles or knew anything about formulas. Indeed, this adoption had given me a new opportunity to pass on new ideas on child care to the women of the area. When it was time to go, the mother's face was very happy. Her baby daughter had come home to visit her, and she had a chance to see that she was well and happy. And she was happy to know I wanted her to keep in touch with her daughter. She gave me a bundle of noodles wrapped in red paper. And then she did what every mother did on a daughter's first visit home; she hung around the baby's neck a red paper package containing a coin for prosperity. This little paper-wrapped coin hung by three threads: a red thread for happiness, a black for youth (black hair), and white for long life (white hair). Then we got into the chair and rode off while the whole family and all the neighbors stood by the gate watching and smiling.

16

I Meet Precious Cloud and His Bandit Gang

PASTOR LAU from Eleventh Town called on me one day, saying that Precious Cloud, the infamous bandit leader of the locality, had put up notices in Eleventh Town streets offering $1,000 reward for the head of General Bing Hu, the local commandant at the county seat. When Bing Hu's soldiers discovered the notices, they seized a man they thought had put them up. "They brought him to my church," said Pastor Lau. "They pushed aside all the seats and tied a rope around one of his thumbs. They threw the rope over a rafter and pulled him aloft. When he fainted with pain, they dropped him with a thud and threw water in his face. When he revived they did it again and again, until he confessed."

I inquired where Precious Cloud and his gang hid.

"Most of his 1,000 followers stay in Twelfth Town, close to the mountains. But sometimes they come into Eleventh Town and stop at our church. There is no method to keep them out."

I knew that this band also crossed over the high mountain between Twelfth and Tenth Towns to terrorize the small villages in that area. Just a few days before, a man had brought his two little sons to the hospital. They came from a small hamlet near Tenth Town. The two little boys were five and eight years old and came to have their lacerated faces repaired. Each child had several deep gashes up to six inches long; every one was cut right down to the bone. "How did this happen?" I asked, as I sewed up cut after cut.

"We could not pay the bandit tax," the father answered sadly.

When the faces had been treated, I examined the boys and found large areas of old scar tissue from burns. "What does this mean?" I asked the father.

"Last year we could not pay our taxes, so Precious Cloud's men wrapped my two sons in straw and set them on fire." His face was white, drawn, desperate. The five-year-old son had lost his mind.

There were other bandit victims among the patients in our very full hospital in 1929. Some had bullet wounds through their arms or legs. One man's leg was smashed to pieces; I told him we would have to amputate. He refused and went home. But after some days he came back with a dreadfully infected leg, begging me to take it off. When we were able to fit in the operation I went to speak to him before we put him under anesthesia. "Will the doctor please postpone the operation?" he asked. "Today is raining and I want my brother here when it is done. He will not be able to come in this weather."

I was irritated, fearing that the American consul might at any time order me out of Mintsing. I wanted to complete the treatment on his leg before I left. But because he insisted, I postponed the operation. In time the sun came out and the brother appeared. I checked the leg once more. It was cleaner and the flesh looked healthier! "Your leg looks a little better," I told him. "Would you like me to wait a few more days and see if it can get well without opening the knife?" That, of course, he was glad to do. The leg continued to improve almost miraculously, and the bones healed in spite of all the infection.

When the day came for him to go home, once again able to walk, tears came to his eyes and he said gratefully, "Doctor has saved me my leg. There is one thing I want to give you to show my happiness. I want to give you my only son." Little did he know how many sons and daughters had been offered to me! I thanked him warmly for the honor thus bestowed but asked him to please raise the boy for me since I wanted him to grow up accustomed to Chinese food and ways.

Then one day an ominous letter arrived. "Will the honorable doctor come right away to see me in Eleventh Town at the church?" This was the gist of the note that was brought by a nondescript messenger from Precious Cloud. Would I travel to his hangout to visit the man who, with his gang of 1,000 men, burned, massacred, and raped as they attacked village after village? Not I.

However I had to be very careful how I answered. One wrong word or sentence could lead to unfortunate consequences, even death. No one was there that day who could advise me, but I could not keep the messenger waiting, for he feared discovery by the local soldiers. I finally told the messenger that no one was there to write a proper letter, so I would give him my answer orally. I would go after the completion of an important operation if I could find chair bearers. At the earliest it would be late in the afternoon. I added, "If there is no chair there is no way to come." Since I did not want to go, I told myself the scarcity of chair bearers would make a good excuse.

In Fukien at that time three rival factions were struggling for supremacy. General Diong Din kept his troops in the southern third of Fukien and controlled the Amoy revenues. The navy controlled Foochow and its environs; with the big naval training station, arsenals, forts and ships, the city was nearly impregnable. In western Fukien, Bandit Lu Hing-bang was supreme. Though he was a man with an infamous reputation, it was said he had been a close friend of Sun Yat-sen. His area of control bordered on that of the communists in Kiangsi. The central government had tried to appease the three factions. It appointed Admiral Yang of the Navy as governor of the province, a friend of Diong Din as Chairman of Public Works, and a friend of Bandit Lu as Collector of Salt Revenues. However, Yang in Foochow and Diong Din in Amoy had put their heads together to devise a way to rid themselves of Bandit Lu. Lu heard of the plans and moved first. A good friend of Lu invited twelve of the most important members of the provincial government to a feast. At the feast Lu's men captured them and took them upriver as captives.

Fortunately General Bing Hu was in Mintsing at this time and did not attend the fatal feast. But at the time I received Precious Cloud's letter, Bing Hu was nevertheless in a tight spot, for Bandit Lu now held Fukien from its western border east to White Sands, between Mintsing and Foochow. Thus Bing Hu's forces were blocked on the west, north, and east. And Precious Cloud, with his "army" of 1,000, blocked any escape to the south. General Bing Hu refused to ally with Bandit Lu, nor would he permit Precious Cloud to join up with him. After all, Precious Cloud had begun as Bing Hu's houseboy.

When Mr. Sia finally returned I showed him Precious Cloud's letter. He was silent for a long time. Then he said, "You *must* go. If you refuse, and if later they take this town, they will punish not only you but all the hospital people."

Early the next morning I left in a chair for the ten-mile ride. When the chair men set me down in the Eleventh Town church, Mr. Hsu, my former teacher and now an ally of Precious Cloud, was on hand to greet me. He was very cordial, and the bandit soldiers (who had tried to kill Dr. Dang when I was in America) were very ceremonious, bowing and scraping and dashing off for cups of hot tea and a basin of hot water for washing. For some reason I felt safer when I found Mr. Hsu was there.

Mr. Hsu had been our pastor during my first term in Mintsing. He was a man of medium height, with shining black eyes and thick lips. He was also something of a scholar. He had loved teaching me Chinese in Mintsing, and I had learned much from him. But even then, although he was in his pulpit Sunday mornings and came to teach me five days a week, I had suspected that he spent some of his nights in bandit activities. When I returned from the United States in December 1928, he met me and warned anxiously about walking alone in Mintsing. In fact, he was warning me to watch out for his own gang. I thanked him politely then and asked him in what duty he was at present engaged. He had replied that he was in government service. Though I had suspected that really meant he was in the service of Precious Cloud, I had nevertheless given him the proper bow of respect.

A strange lame man entered after we had talked for about four hours. Mr. Hsu disappeared when the man showed me a card with Precious Cloud's name on it. I followed him out of the church; we went in a roundabout way through the streets until finally we entered a house. We proceeded to an inner room. Here there was a wide bed, an opium set placed in the middle. In one corner stood a small bed trimmed with lace and a mosquito net. Mr. Hsu then appeared and threw himself on one side of the large bed; my escort lay on the other. They took little black balls of opium and heated them on something like hatpins over a small alcohol lamp. When they were the right consistency, these were put into their long pipes. When these two had finished smoking, two more men came in; and then another pair and another, until twenty men had taken their opium. Meanwhile, a Chinese doctor, apparently deeply disturbed about his own health, sat beside me reciting his symptoms.

Then a young fellow strode into the room, followed by a group of men. Everyone stood at attention. Thus I knew this young man was the chief of the bandits, the infamous Precious Cloud. We sat down for a two-hour feast. I found Precious Cloud to be as shy as a young boy. Every time I spoke to him he blushed. Perhaps Precious Cloud was not so responsible personally for all the wicked deeds that had been perpetrated in his name. Was he simply the puppet of Increased Privilege, an evil-looking man of middle age?

I was the only woman present. There I was in the seat of honor! Why were they honoring me? Why had Precious Cloud sent for me?

Obviously he was no sick man. I thought of the fatal feast in Foochow. Perhaps they wanted to make amends for attacking the hospital, frightening Dr. Dang, and stealing our ponies when I was in America. We talked only of simple things at the table. I dared not say much. There are many double meanings in Chinese and it would not be safe to make a mistake of any kind. In spite of their promise to have me back to Sixth Town by dark, the feast continued into the evening. Since I knew the staff would be worried, Mr. Hsu kindly sent a messenger to inform them I was all right. Though the gang had treated me with great respect during the feast, after the meal they all left with no explanation. Mr. Hsu gave me a room next to his in the church. When I awoke in the morning the bandit soldiers told me that Mr. Hsu was asleep and would not be disturbed. Precious Cloud and many of his men had not yet returned, but I was to wait for him.

Just then my malaria, which always came on in the morning, caught me in its icy clutch. Aching muscles, chattering teeth, violent waves of nausea, a horrible cold that traveled up and down my spine, and all the misery of high fever hit me hard. My face turned white and I was so weak the bandit soldiers had to help me into a chair for the ten-mile trip back to Sixth Town. When I reached the hospital I found the whole staff standing under the camphor tree looking downriver for me. They had been worrying each other over the tortures I might be suffering. Old U Chai had joined them in this and kept repeating, to everyone's dismay, "Boiling her in oil right now." By noon the attack of malaria was over and I was as well as ever. I later learned that all Precious Cloud had wanted from me was a shot for syphilis.

17
Bandits and Soldiers

We awoke one morning late in June 1929, to the sound of rapid gunfire all around us, screaming in the street, and the quick slamming together of shop fronts. Nurses came running, breathless and frightened. "Precious Cloud is coming," they said. "And Bing Hu is running toward Fourth Town with his army."

"Tell every girl and woman to run to their own homes, if they wish," I said quickly, "although I think they might be safer here."

The rattle of machine gun fire downriver was getting nearer. Soon we saw Bing Hu and his little army running through Sixth Town. Sweating, panting, frightened, they ran past our windows with General Bing Hu leading. He had a handkerchief over his mouth, and he was leading his son by the hand as they ran. Through the deserted street they rushed and out on the long shaking bridge, each board thumping as they ran.

Once across the bridge they did not take the usual trail up Ko Iong; they chose a smaller one. "Surely Precious Cloud will have men waiting to catch them on the mountain," I said sadly to Dr. Dang. We watched as the men ran in single file through the paddy fields and as they rapidly climbed the steep trail. Then we spotted bandit soldiers tearing down the regular Ko Iong path. The two forces passed each other without knowing it, and Bing Hu escaped.

The bandits now entered Sixth Town from downriver, from Third Town, and from Ko Iong. At the same time the town's citizenry rushed their women and children out of town. Some were running with precious possessions on their backs. All of the girls at the hospital stayed with us. They reasoned that my gesture in going to treat Precious Cloud, even though I did not succeed, entitled me and the whole staff to special consideration. In their own homes no one would be safe. We kept our gate locked all day. No one went in or out.

All through that mercilessly hot day news kept coming to us.

"They have entered the government school, smashed all the windows, and taken off most everything," a nurse reported breathlessly. We had seen the principal earlier, dressed as a country woman, run across the bridge very soon after the army passed over. The principal was a girl with whom Bing Hu had lived when he was in Sixth Town. Naturally the bandits would wreak terrible revenge on her if they caught her, but she managed to escape.

"They are going right through the village looting everyone," someone else reported later. Far into the night we heard women screaming on the other side of the walls.

The next day the cook asked permission to go home. "My fourteen-year-old niece died at their hands last night," she explained. "I must go home for her funeral."

I looked out the window and saw bandit soldiers leading off long lines of people who were tied together with ropes in single file. Other captives followed carrying big bundles of loot on their shoulders. But no one molested us. It looked as though we were safe, so finally I ordered the gate opened to let in the wounded, including the bandit soldiers, for treatment.

One morning I said to these bandit patients, "Would you like to attend our chapel this morning?" From the horrified looks on the faces of the staff I could see that they considered this an awful mistake. But something had told me to ask them, and I was sure it was right. Thus, thirty bandit soldiers attended our chapel service and conducted themselves with propriety.

Sometime later even Precious Cloud came in for treatment, accompanied by the former Pastor Hsu and his bodyguard. I learned that Mr. Hsu was now taking $10 to $14 worth of opium daily. This meant he was heading for real trouble, for his income surely could not long cover the cost of his growing needs. I was sad that this young man had so squandered his life. At the same time it seemed a curious twist of fate that he was protecting so many lives within our walls even while he ruined his own.

During that hot summer of 1929 we saw and experienced great hardship. Food was scarce; salt was running out; our kerosene would not last much longer. Fortunately, we had a fair supply of medicine. But the constant blasting heat, the relentless fear we felt for our own lives and others', and the limited diet of rice without salt made it a difficult time for all. But luckily for us, when it came time for people to get rid of their ducks, which could not get through to the Foochow markets, we had duck to add to the rice and vegetables. Also, sometimes a boy brought us a string of frogs. Later farmers brought hard green peaches, which we could eat when cooked. But that was the extent of our menus through the rest of June, July, August, and September 1929.

The local people had it even worse than we in the compound. People came weeping to me about the heavy taxes. Precious Cloud demanded exorbitant taxes just after General Bing Hu had cleaned them out with his "military taxes." People committed suicide because they could not pay. If they did not fork out the tax the people could expect torture; and they were shot on the slightest pretext. Even though I was told Precious Cloud would not harm me or the hospital, the same people warned me that some of his men might nevertheless attempt to kidnap me for ransom. I was told to be very careful.

We knew that a band of soldiers, purportedly communists, had captured Miss Harrison and Miss Nelleman, two missionaries further upriver. We heard they were being tortured daily while the soldiers waited for ransom money. The soldiers had cut off one of Miss Harrison's fingers and sent it to Foochow with the demand for a big ransom. I saw the finger, carefully preserved in a bottle at Magaw Hospital, some time later. Some Chinese friends of mine seemed to know some details of the torture; they told me that Miss Harrison had already lost her mind. Later we heard that both women had been killed.

Even the outside world knew about the Stams incident further north. Mrs. Stams was raped repeatedly, her husband tied to the foot of the bed, and both were beheaded. They had managed to slip their baby out of sight, however, so it was saved. Other missionaries had been taken in various places, so indeed there was a reason to worry. Consequently, the American consul at Foochow ordered all of the local missionaries to leave at once for the county seat. He had chartered a special launch which possessed a permit to cross the line of battle on the Min River in order to collect all missionaries upriver and transport them to Foochow. I refused to leave the hospital, however, when so much needed to be done at that time, so I did not join the exodus. But when Mr. Sia and others informed me of a plot to kidnap me, I finally consented to go to the county seat for a few days to wait for Bing Hu's forces to restore order.

One day while we waited at the county seat a long line of women, escorted by Precious Cloud's men, came walking into town. We learned that Precious Cloud sent his men to seize seventy women and girls in Third Town. These women had been forced to march more than twenty miles through the awful heat. Some were pregnant, some had just had babies, some had bound feet, and others were just little girls. On the way a number could go no further, so the soldiers had shot twenty of them. Three more had been beaten to death. It seemed like a bad dream.

On September 10, 1929, we received word that things had calmed down in Sixth Town. My friend, Third Aunt, engaged a boat without saying anything about me. At dawn the next day I got into the boat and lay flat in it all day until we returned to Sixth Town. No sooner had I arrived than a letter came from Increased Privilege, Precious Cloud's henchman, asking me to go to Eleventh Town to treat a sick woman.

I had gone to see Increased Privilege one day after returning from the visit with Precious Cloud in Eleventh Town. He had an evil-looking face. His wife, who had been my patient, had been in Foochow earlier with her two small sons. When Increased Privilege set fire to the official's house in Fifteenth Town and burned him and his wife at the stake, a political foe in Foochow caught Increased Privilege's wife and sons and threw them into prison in reprisal. They were in prison for ten months. She told me later that during that time they had no water for washing and that the room was kept pitch black. She and the children had spent the whole time on the bed because the floor was covered with filth. When Bandit Lu had seized the important men at the Foochow feast, he also managed to get Increased Privilege's wife and sons out of prison. The wife was too weak to walk, and I found later that she had beriberi. I wanted very much to see the sons, wondering how they had fared, but never had the opportunity. Now Increased Privilege was calling me to see some sick woman in Eleventh Town.

I was afraid and did not want to go, but I decided to get the best advice and follow it. Cung Dai's face turned white, and his eyes got big and dark when I showed him the letter. "You cannot go," he said violently. Mr. Sia agreed.

Then Cung Dai went to the Sixth Town yamen and asked one of Precious Cloud's officers whether he thought I should go. "By no means should she go," he answered.

So it was settled that Cung Dai would go in my place. That night he returned with the sick woman. She was Increased Privilege's mistress, but she was also a relative of Precious Cloud's father. Precious Cloud's father felt that his family had been disgraced by this illicit affair, so he hired someone to beat her. The hired man had done his job well; she had been beaten over the head and face with an iron bar.

Meanwhile, Precious Cloud was beginning to feel the pinch as he rubbed against other bases of power. He had tried to join Bing Hu's forces, but the latter shot to death each messenger who attempted to deliver the bandit's letters. Then Precious Cloud sent secret messengers to offer his services and men to General Lau in Foochow, but again the messengers were shot. Bandit Lu agreed to take him in only if he would promise to send a terrific amount of supplies. But Precious Cloud was unable to produce such large amounts of supplies. Then Bandit Lu took the county seat, and Precious Cloud retreated to Eleventh Town.

At six o'clock in the evening on September 24, 1929, we heard the firing of guns from the direction of Third Town. We expected that Bing Hu would return from that direction. But Cung Dai ran over and told us to keep out of sight because these invaders might be quite wild. We closed all the windows, pulled furniture against closed doors, collected bundles of bedding, and moved over to the office at the center of the compound. We all huddled there, shaking with fear. Now the firing was very near, accompanied by fiendish, blood-curdling screams. It sounded as though hordes were descending on us. Bullets screeched over our buildings, flames burst from guns, and the air smelled of gunpowder. I sneaked over to a window. Men were racing on the street. Then Precious Cloud's hundred soldiers came piling out of the yamen as the screaming, shooting fiends approached. With no time to fire back, the bandits of Precious Cloud ran as hard as they could downriver toward White Cloud Ferry, where Precious Cloud hid.

The next morning we learned that only twenty of Bing Hu's men had invaded Sixth Town the previous night, but they had had the cooperation of citizens all the way from Third to Sixth Town. Everyone stood in the gate of his home and shot off his gun as fast as he could. The hundred bandits had heard the guns of perhaps a thousand men. They had left so fast that they took nothing with them, not even their poor women.

The next day we witnessed a most amazing sight. Every path all over the valley was crowded with women and children traveling home in single file. After almost four months away, families returned rejoicing. Women came with children on their backs and in their arms; more children trudged along behind. Some came with the babies born during their exile. Some were heavily laden with the clothes and kettles they had taken with them. It was a day of happiness after four months of separation from their men folk who had stayed to protect their homes in the face of torture or death. Some returned to find their husbands or sons dead. But all had come back to pick up the threads of life that remained.

For the next two days the local conquering heroes, Bing Hu's forces, poured into Sixth Town in little groups. They were dressed in ragged peasant clothes, with straw hats and straw sandals; some had guns. One man wore a washbasin on his head, and many more wore towels wrapped tightly around their heads. They were a motley, undis-

Up the Mighty Min River

The Mintsing Hospital

Harvesting Rice

Crossing a Horse-Tooth Bridge

A Season for Kites

Bandits with Captured Women

An Outdoor Operation

Warlord Soldiers Marching Through Mintsing

Trackers on the Yangtze

Priests in a Local Ceremony of Atonement

Street Life in Chungking

Fleeing to the River, Chungking

ciplined lot. They appeared to be just as dangerous as Precious Cloud's men. They began immediately to take revenge on anyone who had had good relations with Precious Cloud. We saw some very shocking sights from behind our closed shutters.

On the last day of September a mysterious messenger brought a letter that asked me to go at once to see a very sick man in Eleventh Town. It was not signed in Chinese. Mr. Hsu had scrawled his name in English. Cung Dai told me not to go, for Precious Cloud's men were ready to retreat further to the south. He worried that this would be an ideal time to seize me for ransom. Another said that General Bing Hu would be terribly angry if I went to treat one of his enemies. But since I was willing to treat anyone, this was not a convincing argument for me. In the end Mr. Sia also warned of a possible kidnapping, so I told the messenger I was very busy with hospital work and could find no transportation. This was a lie, but it was an accepted Chinese way of dealing with the situation. A few days later another urgent letter came. It told me to go to Eleventh Town to wait for someone. No name was given, probably for fear that the messenger would be shot if the letter revealed bandit connections.

This time Mr. Sia said, "If you do not go, and if ever Precious Cloud takes this town again, you and your hospital will be severely punished." So I had to go. I was glad to have Cung Dai go with me. Because Bing Hu would punish us if he knew, we obtained chairs secretly and were off.

Along the road people politely asked where we were going. "Down the river," Cung Dai would say, or, "to the next village."

When we arrived in Eleventh Town we found the church was closed. A strange emptiness and silence pervaded the street. Finally Pastor Lau appeared and opened the gate for us. He led us silently to his study. "My wife, my daughter, the Bible women, the teachers, and all other women in the town have gone into hiding," he said gravely. Cung Dai explained why we were there, but Pastor Lau knew nothing.

Cung Dai then wandered through the town and finally met a

bright-looking young officer. "Does anyone want a doctor?" he asked.

"I will inquire and let you know," the officer replied, and off he went.

Eventually he came to the church and said "they" were collecting the sick in one place for me to see. We waited two hours before the man returned. He led us in a very roundabout manner through the town, going through one house after another until at last we came to a low, dark room.

Wounded men lay all over the floor. There were no mats or mosquito nets. One man had a terrible wound on his shoulder; the bone was badly shattered. We moved him to the church, where I had him placed on a door which we put on two sawhorses to serve as an operating table. We used a wide window ledge as a scrub table; the pulpit became the instrument table. Cung Dai administered chloroform while I did a debridement* and put on a clean dressing. A male nurse, who had practiced as a doctor in Eleventh Town for a number of years and who was now in Precious Cloud's service, watched the operation. I told him how to change dressings daily. He was ghastly white with fear. It looked as though he expected to be shot if the man were to die in his hands.

When all of the cases had been treated, we were dreadfully hungry. The officer said he would take us to food. When he led us into a room where Increased Privilege was sitting, however, we quickly lost our appetites. He received us coldly. We had to sit down with a half-circle of evil-looking men who had such dreadful expressions in their eyes that I was nauseated. Roasted chestnuts were passed around, but our mouths were too dry to swallow them. My feet were like ice. Cung Dai's face became whiter and whiter, and his eyes grew bigger until at last his face seemed to be shrinking. Every few minutes Increased Privilege burst into a rage about something, yelling violently. We two victims sat in a circle

* The removal by surgery of dead or damaged tissue, as well as all foreign matter, from a wound.

for a full hour without saying anything. Someone brought us each a bowl of watery rice with pork and squash. We both made an effort to make a dent in the rice. Then someone mentioned chair money and the doctor's fee to Increased Privilege. He burst into a frightful rage. The circle of eyes watched his every move and said not a word. At last he pulled out his money drawer and took out a handful of dollars. But then he hurled the money back into the drawer and locked it. I knew then that he would let us go but would not pay us.

I then said to Increased Privilege my first words in the whole two hours' session. "If only we had good roads, I could drive a car over here; then we would not have to pay for chair coolies." This was the Chinese way of saying, "If only you had not taken our ponies . . ." I dared not look at Cung Dai, for he must have been in collapse at such a remark.

We finally said our farewells and they let us go. We were wretchedly hungry but dared not stop in the street to buy cookies, for fear the gang leader would change his mind and stop us. As usual on such trips, although no one else knew it, I had two grains of morphine hidden in my clothes in case worse came to worst. Again it was not needed.

Soon after that trek to treat the bandits I decided to visit Foochow, taking the baby, Hwa Sing, with me. Foochow seemed like another world, in contrast to the trying conditions we experienced that summer. It seemed wonderful until I found that no accommodations were available to me with Hwa Sing along. Even the people at Magaw Hospital said I would be welcome if only I had not brought a Chinese baby. It was very hard for me to digest the fact that those who came to "convert the heathen" could show such discrimination. After all the hard experiences and isolation of the last four months, this was a blow. I was bitter, but I did need rest; so Mary Carleton kindly took Hwa Sing, while I lived with my Western colleagues. I felt that all missionaries ought to undergo psychoanalysis to root out whatever feelings of racial superiority might lurk in their subconscious before they were allowed to preach

Christianity in China. People had described the Chinese as rigid traditionalists. But they could not be more rigid than some of our "good" missionaries in the field.

It was during that stay in Foochow that I met Esther and Olin Stockwell, who were now being assigned by the bishop to join me in Mintsing. Esther was a highly intelligent girl and very understanding person. She played the piano beautifully. Olin was a young man who had already impressed me several months before when he had visited Sixth Town. He was able to relate easily with the Chinese and enjoyed their food. Their two blonde, blue-eyed children would also help brighten our life in Sixth Town.

Also while I was resting in Foochow, Stephen returned from his year of study in Peiping. He brought with him a female police dog, five kinds of rabbits, imported piglets, purebred white goats, ducks, chickens, strawberry plants and a number of other things. He also brought me a variety of serums from Peking Union Medical College, where he had studied.* His conversations were all about laboratory work and about the various projects he was planning in order to help the Mintsing farmers. He was happy to be returning to put his knowledge into practice. Hwa Sing and I took a boat back to Mintsing with Stephen and his menagerie.

When we arrived back in Sixth Town we learned that Increased Privilege, Mr. Hsu, and Precious Cloud had escaped to Ing Tai, where they were said to have become high officials in the Nanking government. Hundreds of the old gang members remained, however, and they were said to be gathering in Tenth Town and Twelfth Town. Some people thought they might be planning to take our town again. Meanwhile, Bandit Lu had retreated into Kiangsi Province, where it was said he joined the communists.

The rumor about Precious Cloud proved true. Not long after our

* Officially opened in September 1921, in the presence of John D. Rockefeller, Jr., the Rockefeller-supported Peking Union Medical College in Peiping became the foremost medical institution in China.

return to Sixth Town, Precious Cloud returned to Mintsing in triumph. He had joined the Nationalist troops in Ing Tai and was now a member of Chiang Kai-shek's army. General Bing Hu could not fight him now, for ostensibly, at least, they were on the same side. Former Pastor Hsu had done some clever planning, and it appeared that he had outwitted General Bing Hu.

18

A Local Ceremony of Atonement

"WOULD THE DOCTOR like to go with us to see *Puo Do?*" Cung Dai, now married, appeared at the door to ask me to go with a number of the staff. We traveled along the little path upriver, across Eighteenth Fair Bridge to a little village where everything had been prepared for the occasion. *Puo Do* meant "crossing place." Everyone passed there when he left this world. In certain cases, however, something might prevent some of the souls from crossing. Since it was an expensive undertaking to transport these souls across, a small village saved its money for several years before putting on the ceremony. In the case of this village it had been around seventy years since a *Puo Do* ceremony had been held. So it was my good fortune to attend the rites of atonement for past sins that had kept certain souls from making the crossing during the past seven decades.

Outside the temple high platforms had been arranged on each side of the path. Scenes made of paper were set up on these platforms. Paper shops and paper people were all arranged realistically. We looked inside of some of the village's shops and homes. Pasted on the walls of some of them were pictures of foreign men and women, and one showed a man and woman kissing. In those days in China this was considered highly improper, so this picture drew the biggest number of onlookers. When I appeared they all muttered, thinking who knows what thoughts. Of course, I tried to look properly shocked.

On the other side of the street were placed booths which portrayed the punishments of hell. Strings attached to the figures of sinners, pulled by children under the platforms, caused them to jump in agony. In one booth a black-faced man violently paddled a prone sinner. In another two men vigorously sawed a sinner in two. In yet another two men were vigorously sawing a man from top to bottom. A horse-headed human in another booth pulled a sinner up and down inside a red hot chimney; the victim had been roasted browner than a Thanksgiving turkey. It gave me the creeps. Further on, green-faced employees of hell fried a victim in a great kettle of oil. In another booth a group of demons were dropping a heavy weight with a bang on the poor sinner's belly, squashing him flat. In the last booth the sinner had been jammed into a mill head first, with only his legs sticking out, while two administrators of hellish justice ground the mill on and on. Where history runs so far back, who could guess whether priests first conceived these punishments and so inspired bandits; or did ancient bandit atrocities furnish priests with ideas to threaten people into being good? I was reminded of Foxe's book of martyrs* in the Western tradition.

The temple was a blaze of glory. Lovely silk Chinese lanterns with wooden frames hung everywhere, some in the shape of temples, while others were fashioned into pagodas. Beautifully elaborate gold tapestries hung in a solid mass over the wall behind the altar. "Each is worth several tens of dollars," the girls whispered to me. Someone else added that they were lent by Drum Mountain Monastery.† Large paintings hung on both side walls as well as on the rear wall of the temple's interior. Two depicted the sufferings of the wicked, but also the blessings meted out to the good. The good people were arranged in family groups; they

* John Foxe, *Actes and Monuments of these Latter and Perilous Dayes* (1563).

† This large Buddhist establishment was located on Drum Mountain, about ten miles northeast of Foochow, and was famous for its relic tooth of the Buddha. An early Protestant missionary, William H. Medhurst, had little success convincing the resident monks that their treasure was in fact an elephant's tooth.

sat with contented faces and enjoyed eating on tables set among hills, with trees and waterfalls nearby and with mountains in the background. The sinners were all alone and suffered the same gruesome punishments portrayed in the booths outside.

Monks in red gowns stood against the golden tapestries by the altar and sang in cadences, accompanied by string and wind instruments. It was beautiful, and I wished that I could somehow capture this gorgeously exotic picture for people in America to see. When we emerged into the night a fire blazed in a great kettle held on a tripod. With the flames throwing weird, phantomlike images, it provided just the right touch to end a beautifully mystical evening.

Later, another *Puo Do* was held in a small village just downriver from Sixth Town. Again some of us went. The temple service had finished by the time we arrived. About twenty priests in red robes then filed out to the open space in front of the temple. As they came out single file, they sang charmingly in a minor key. Each carried two lighted paper lanterns and slowly they circled around a fire that blazed in a tripod set in the center of the yard. Bells, drums, flutes, and stringed instruments opened up a lively concert. The priests quickened their pace to the time of the music and broke into a dance around the fiery cauldron, raising and lowering their arms. Their lighted yellow lanterns rose and fell rhythmically as they circled the fire in harmony with the music. The orchestra quickened its time and the red-robed monks bobbed faster and faster. Then the music became wildly fast, and the yellow lanterns and red robes moved in and out in intricate patterns, faster and faster, until it seemed the colors had merged. I thought of mad butterflies as I watched them.

In the end the priests crushed their lighted lanterns and hurled them high into the air. The crowd then stormed furiously into their midst and struggled violently to catch a lantern, believing this would bring good luck for a whole year. By this time I was so much taken by the spirit of the ceremony I almost wanted to tear in with them. This was followed by a ceremony in which rice and clothes were distributed to beggars. I was deeply grateful for having been permitted to see so much beauty. I wondered how many more unusual and worthwhile events I would see during my time in Mintsing.

19

The End of Precious Cloud, and Bing Hu's Affairs

IN NOVEMBER 1930, the soldiers had caught Precious Cloud, apparently no longer protected by his affiliation with the Nationalist government. But he outwitted them at the very end for he, too, carried a lethal dose of opium and swallowed it before they began the torture. I felt sorry. I wondered about Mr. Hsu. Since no one would tell me anything about his fate I suspected that it must have been too ghastly to repeat to me because we had been friends. Thus, two able young men had chosen the wrong path and had paid for it with their lives. And their families would continue to pay a bitter price.

Increased Privilege did not get off so easily, but I wasted no pity on him. One of the last things I had heard about him was that he had filled a coffin full of his ill-gotten tax money; then he took two soldiers off somewhere to bury it. When the coffin had been carefully buried in a secret place, he shot both of the soldiers so that no one would know where the money was hidden. When Increased Privilege was caught, he was sent to Third Town to be punished by the women there. He had been responsible for the seizure of the seventy women from that town, so the judgment seemed apt. The women decided on death by the shoe awl. They first tied him in a chair. Then the women went into his room in a never-ending procession. Each carried her sharp shoe awl. They pierced him with the awls hour after hour, night and day for three days till he was finally dead.

After Christmas dinner, 1930, we went to church to hear General Bing Hu speak. I was not thrilled with his highly moral message. I remembered what his soldiers had done to the man in Eleventh Town church. I also thought of our ponies which he had captured from Precious Cloud, but had not returned to us. I thought of the harmless old deaf man who supplied our hospital; Bing Hu's soldiers clubbed him to death in front of me and the children because his son was thought to have been in Precious Cloud's army. I thought of the poppy seeds Bing Hu sold to the local people at $10 for each winecup full. He also collected a high tax on the growing poppies. When the crop was nearly mature he would send his soldiers around to pull it up, scolding the farmers for growing opium—that is, if he had not been paid off, for other fields went untouched and bountiful harvests of opium were reaped.

A patient of mine, once mayor at the county seat, told me that Bing Hu had cleared $200,000 during his forty months in Mintsing. Much of this came from soldiers' salaries, given to him by the government, but not passed on to the intended recipients. This was a time-honored means powerful men in the old China used. The poor soldiers were paid only four month's wages in three years. The general also received tax money from all the boats that came upriver from Foochow. He taxed the little creek boats in our locality $3 per month; there were between 500 and 700 such boats in the county. He made roughly $3,000 per month in the opium racket. About 600 ounces of opium were smuggled in over the mountain trails from Hinghua every month; the general made $5 on every ounce. My patient had related other sources of income, but I could not keep all of it in my head until I reached my diary. I thought of all this during the Christmas sermon in our church.

But before I went to sleep that night my thoughts shifted to the new road that General Bing Hu had been building. This road would connect the county seat to Sixth Town. It was now almost half done. Some enterprising citizens had already bought an old bus for $1,000 and were making from $50 to $55 per day carrying passengers over as much of the road as had been finished. Already I had written to the church headquarters in America. I told them about the new road and reminded them that, years before, a friend of Dr. Carleton's had left $1,000 to buy a windmill for the hospital. Since we no longer needed a windmill, I asked to be allowed to use the gift money for a car. My Christmas gift that year was a positive response from the mission headquarters. Before I went to sleep that night I resolved to use my next summer's vacation to go to Shanghai to find a good secondhand car. With rapid and dependable transportation between Sixth Town and the county seat, we could bring good medical service to both places.

When summer 1931, came, Magaw Hospital asked me to come to work there. I had written back that I guessed I would not be able to come. Then they wrote that I could bring my children, so we packed up and headed for Foochow. At the end of August the children and I left Foochow to attend medical meetings in Shanghai, to make a visit to Nanchang, and to bring back a car. That September, the two girls and I boarded a dirty old ship in Shanghai for the trip back to Foochow. The rats were so terrible that I had to take Hwa Sing into bed with me. All night I had to fight the rats off the bed. But in the hold, oblivious to the rats, stood a secondhand Ford. I named it Robin, since it had a black top and a dark red body.

20

Medical Service by Automobile

DURING THE FALL DAYS of 1931, Olin Stockwell taught me how to drive the car, so I then was able to go by car from the county seat to Third Town. When the rains made the clay roads more slippery than ice, Olin kindly drove me. Now I could seriously consider taking up work at the little hospital in the county seat in addition to the work at Sixth Town. So in January 1932, Cung Dai and his wife Moon Lily, Hwa Sing, and I moved to the empty mission house at the Boys' School in the county seat. Hwa Hui had to stay in Sixth Town with Dr. Dang to attend the Girls' School. We cleaned up the dirty mission house and gathered enough furniture to open a small hospital. Cung Dai and Moon Lily became the superintendents.

The county seat was a town of rich and influential people who could pay well for medical services. They were well enough informed to have respect for Western medicine. Our business thrived from the start, and we were busy night and day. Thus, the work at the county seat began to aid our medical effort in the back country. It became a pattern of my life to constantly shuttle back and forth between the county seat and Sixth Town. More and more I felt the need for Dr. Huang but now she could not come.

One day in March 1932, when I was at Sixth Town and Dr. Dang was on vacation, the telephone which Bing Hu had connected between the two towns called me to the county seat. It was pouring rain, so Olin offered to drive me. He had to put chains on the tires because the mud was so slippery. The ruts were so deep that the center scraped the car's belly much of the way. "I've seen worse roads than this in Oklahoma," said Olin cheerfully when I expressed my dismay.

When we reached the hospital we found that Cung Dai's baby girl was very sick with meningitis. I thought we had better take her to Sixth Town, where we had better equipment. It was dark when we got back. Cung Dai and Moon Lily carefully carried the baby to my residence where I could watch her through the night. Moon Lily went to bed exhausted, but Cung Dai came over to eat with me. Before eating he bowed his head and prayed aloud, "Please spare her life. But whatever is Your will, let it be done."

This moved me profoundly. He had such faith in what he called God. Though he adored his baby girl, he was accepting her death if it was to be. I knew that he was utterly sincere. He had a missionary-taught faith in God and believed that if his daughter died, God was taking her. I would be very careful to do nothing to disturb his faith, so deep and necessary for him at that time. I almost wished I had such a faith. Early the next morning his dear little girl was dead. His grief was deep and heartbreaking in spite of his spirit of acceptance. What could I say to comfort him? Moon Lily too was prostrate with grief. I could not pretend the usual platitudes, including the statement that God had taken her home. No God would take such a sweet baby from her parents. Her death was caused by a disease which I had not been able to cure. I could only silently share their grief and sorrow and try to take care of them.

On one of my many medical excursions that spring we visited a leper colony whose residents came from the villages of the county. At first the lepers were afraid to be seen, but finally one man and then another crept out from a dark corner. They wore looks of utter hopelessness on their faces. Hands and feet were contracted, withered and distorted beyond description. Then, one by one, about ten more limped or shuffled out and stood in a disconsolate circle around us. We asked to see their rooms and found each one to be absolutely dark; each contained a bed and a small stove. Since there was no communal cooking, each man had to shuffle to the hills to find a small armful of wood for fuel, to the well to draw his water, and then to his dismal room to cook his own meal.

The local government had built this edifice many years before. No medical care of any sort had been provided. Because it was eighteen miles from the Sixth Town hospital, we had been unable to make the necessary visits to give treatment. But now there was a road, a car, and a hospital at the county seat. So we could now begin to do something for these miserable men and women who were doomed to live together under such horrible conditions.

While we talked, more lepers appeared until we counted eighteen men and two women. One of the women was in her forties. She was totally blind and shared her room with a man who came from a family of means. This man deeply loved her. When I urged him to take treatments, he refused. I knew why. Since her case was hopeless, he would not be cured and leave her behind. The other female was a lovely young girl whom I had known in Sixth Town. Her mother-in-law hated her and had brought her to the Sixth Town hospital, asking us to send her to this place because she was a leper. We had explained that she had tinea,* not leprosy. But, without my knowing it until this time, she took the girl to the head of her clan and told him the girl had leprosy. The clan head then ordered her sent to the leper colony. She was fourteen when she came to the colony, and one of the men with nodular leprosy had claimed her. She shared his dark room and stove and was now beginning to show nodules on her face.

As I sat looking at the twenty people who had been sent there by their clan heads, I was once again appalled at the consequences of ignorance. Though Mintsing people felt very competent to diagnose leprosy (and actually they were very clever at it), sometimes they mistook syphilis, tuberculosis, or tinea for it. In the case of women, some were shipped to leper colonies simply because they were not wanted. I could hardly bear to look at them in their hopelessness. They had nothing to stimulate them, mentally or spiritually. They were merely trying to get through life by begging rice, growing a few vegetables, garnering a little firewood, and then going to bed. What could be done to combat their apathy and demoralization?

I began to tell them about the people in Sixth Town whom we were curing. I told them that treatment might even help in the advanced stages and offered to come once a week to care for them. But I also made it clear that they would have to be very patient and take treatments week after week and month after month. I told them that with such longterm treatment they would begin to notice a change in their health. The nodules would begin to shrink and the strength would begin to come back to their legs. They brightened as an infinitesimal ray of hope seemed to touch their faces for a moment. They promised to take the long treatment, but I knew they would not all. At least we had to give them the chance, and perhaps one or two would accept the challenge.

* A fungous skin disease such as ringworm.

21

Rumors of Communists, and the Coming of Soldiers

I WAS VERY BUSY in the spring of 1932 when a man arrived from Water Mouth with a telegram from Foochow. Dr. Dang was on vacation, and I was constantly moving between the two hospitals. The telegram came from the American consul and ordered me to proceed to Foochow if I thought conditions warranted it. I thought that I was in no position to know when to go, so I simply put the telegram aside. I did know, however, that people from upriver were pouring into Mintsing, frightened and shaken, telling stories of narrow escapes and bloody deaths of people who had been caught with money. The communists were now in Fukien and were said to be approaching Everlasting Peace, a town at the head of the Min River. The word "communist" was whispered behind hands from one person to another, just as they had spoken previously of Precious Cloud and his gang. All of the missionaries had already moved out.

Then one day when I arrived at the county seat I found Olin waiting for me. I knew at once why he had come. "The consul sent me up to bring you out," he said smiling. I felt ashamed to have caused so much trouble, but was not sure I should go with him. He did not argue. Instead he sat around all the long morning and half the afternoon while I treated patients. Then we drove into Sixth Town where we consulted Mr. Sia, Cung Dai, Stephen, and others who had guided me safely through the bandit days.

"It is not likely the communists will come this far," said Mr. Sia.

"You can put on Chinese clothes and escape with us," said another.

Somehow I felt that I wanted to go. I was tired of danger, and I was afraid. Yet something told me not to go. The talk went back and forth. Olin had come a long way to take me out. I had disobeyed the consul during the dangerous days of Precious Cloud and perhaps should not cross him again. But even that was not sufficient reason for disobeying the voice within that told me to stay. I was afraid, and I wanted to go. That was the deciding factor. Though I kept still, I think the intuitive Chinese could almost read my mind. "It is true that you could not disguise yourself sufficiently to fool the communists," said Mr. Sia. So I gathered a few things together and we started for the county seat, again leaving my two girls with someone who would love and care for them in case I did not get back. Hwa Hui's face was anxious and pale as I left, but young Hwa Sing waved me a gay good-bye.

After only two days of rest at Drum Mountain, outside Foochow, a telegram came calling me back to Mintsing immediately. I left at once. Four chair men ran me down the mountain in record time and rushed me through the streets of Foochow. Soon after I climbed aboard the upriver launch, packed with panting humanity. The launch was so full that I had to ride on the bamboo roof. It was bitter cold after the sun set. Next to me lay a Chinese man in a thin cotton shirt and trousers. So I flipped my blanket over him too, and we toasted each other's backs all night; we would have suffered otherwise. In the morning when he left at a station below mine, although we had said not a word to each other, he threw me the most grateful glance I have ever seen.

People on the boat were worrying that the communists would get to Mintsing before us. When we arrived at ten in the morning, however, they had not yet come, but the town was packed with government soldiers who had come overland from Ing Tai. They were on their way upriver to drive the communists back. I made my way through the hordes to the hospital.

"I have arrived," I said. "What important business is there?"

"We called you for an obstetrical case," Moon Lily said. "We could not deliver her. We tried our best. We finally gave her pituitrin and she died."

They had done their best. But they had ruptured her uterus by giving pituitrin. I had sacrificed a life by running away.

I left the hospital for awhile and went to the empty Boys' School residence where I sat on the porch in the dark. I remembered that before Olin took me to Foochow something had told me not to go. I now became convinced it was necessary to listen to that inner voice, whatever its origin. I vowed never again to disobey this "inner light." I sat in the dark, very sad. Then Cung Dai appeared with a hot bowl of noodles which he had carried in the dark all the way from the hospital. He always knew when I was in trouble and showed his sympathy in some very quiet and unassuming way. He sat on the railing while I ate the noodles. I had to eat them if he stayed.

The next day the communists arrived at Water Mouth, thirty miles upriver. People again urged me to leave. Cung Dai tried his best to get me off. More letters arrived from the consul in Foochow. But I would not budge. Some days later people warned that the communists would arrive that night and that there would be a big battle. Over 100 of the citizens left their homes in the county seat and climbed the nearby hill to spend the night. From there they could easily escape should the communists come. Many more people hired boats and moved downriver to sleep outside the town.

That same night one of our patients went into labor. Moon Lily sat with her, and we waited while listening to the sounds of people outside the windows rushing this way and that. Then came a deadly silence, the silence of a deserted city. The baby finally arrived at midnight. Still no communists; only rumors.

Late in the summer of 1932, Dr. Dang returned along with the missionaries. Things were beginning to go back to normal. Dr. Dang took over the Sixth Town hospital. Hwa Hui went back to school, while Hwa Sing and I lived at the county seat, where we were joined by Olin and his family. The evening after their arrival Olin read *John Brown's Body* to Esther and me while we busily darned stockings.

But this did not mean that Fukien was living in peace and quiet. During the autumn of 1933, the Nineteenth Route Army seized Foochow from the central government and urged other provinces to join in forming the United States of China. The central government sent five airplanes to attack Foochow. Soon the Nineteenth Route Army retreated up the Min River. Foochow again came under the control of Chiang Kai-shek's troops. But the Nineteenth then took over an area that extended from White Sands, below Mintsing, nearly to Yen-p'ing. Some of the Nineteenth's troops joined the communists. All transportation to Foochow was stopped.

Several thousand soldiers poured into the county seat under the command of Bandit Lu, now an honored officer in Chiang Kai-shek's army. The hills around us were covered with machine guns and men. Troops from Nanking had also marched overland for forty days to take Water Mouth. The Nineteenth was bottled up now between White Sands and Water Mouth. Beyond Water Mouth loomed the communist forces, while more government troops had moved into Ing Tai to cut off any southern retreat. The Nineteenth Route Army, which had distinguished itself while fighting the Japanese in Shanghai some months before, was doomed.

Thousands of dirty, weary troops from Nanking marched into the county seat to relieve Bandit Lu. They had traveled so fast from Nanking that they had not washed their clothes, and they had found very little food in the villages they passed through. When the hungry men poured into the town we did not have enough rice to feed our own citizens. But before long they were on the march again, passing through Sixth Town, on their way to Ing Tai to cut off every possible path of retreat for the Nineteenth Route Army. All day long the road was jammed with tired marching men. Many of them were sick; some of them lay down by the roadside able to go no further. Ponies, donkeys, and mules carried cannon and cannon carriages as far as the road went. Then the men had to carry the cumbersome implements of war over mountain trails and steep stone staircases.

As more government troops moved into the county seat I became acquainted with a young commander who had a personal interest in all of his soldiers. One day he came to me and reported that he had over 100 men sick with malaria. The men came from Honan, Anhwei, and

Shantung, provinces which knew no malaria. Now, in addition to the exhausting march, severe exposure, and change of diet, many had succumbed to severe malarial attacks. I told him to send the men to us, the worst ones first, until the beds were filled.

These soldiers were extremely ill. One had a temperature of 107. The nurses and I sat on the floor in a circle around a kerosene lantern making more quilts for the patients. We pulled old tablecloths out of missionary boxes and used them to line some of our quilts. But in the end we were short one. I pulled out my great-grandmother's quilt for the last shivering patient. My great-grandmother had made it for me when I was a very small girl, and I had so adored it that I would permit no one to use it. When I went to China I took it along. It was made up of pieces of cloth cut in blocks; its edging, and lines through it, were turkey red. Now it had found its use.

22

Stephen's Agricultural Work, a Mongolian Pony for Medical Service, and a Holocaust

THE YEARS 1933 and 1934 were filled with activity as I dashed back and forth between the two hospitals in the old car.

Bandits still caused problems. Another military commander had settled in with his men at the county seat, and they had begun a zealous bandit-chasing program. One day they rushed to Fourth Town, where they surrounded a house which harbored bandits, but the bandits had wisely provided themselves with captive farmers. When the soldiers set fire to the thatched roof, the bandits forced the farmers to climb up and put out the fire. The poor farmers had to climb up. They shouted to the soldiers outside that they were farmers, not bandits, but the soldiers knew only Mandarin and hurled grenades at them. Seven innocent farmers were torn to pieces, while all but three bandits escaped. All three were decapitated and their heads were hung in the marketplace as a warning to others.

Despite the still uncertain political situation, Stephen kept steadily and happily at his laboratory experiments and worked his fertile fields across the creek in Sixth Town. There he had built himself a nice little house where he, Fragrant Sister, his baby boy and dog lived. He had developed a good herd of goats and hired a goat boy to take them to pasture every day. He also wanted to introduce white pigs to Mintsing, for they grew much larger than the native black pigs and would produce many more pounds of pork. He bought a white pig and brought it to Sixth Town, but it got so badly sunburned the project had to be abandoned. Even the white spots on the Holstein heifer burned to some degree in the searing heat of Fukien's sun. But she was already larger than the native yellows cows, so Stephen continued to be optimistic about this project. He had also tried to get the local farmers to raise white chickens; they laid approximately double the number of eggs of the native fowl, but the farmers considered white to be the color of mourning and death, and they refused to adopt the new breed. Stephen had given a hatching to each preacher in the hope that the local sentiment would work against tradition once the farmers saw others getting 120 eggs per year from each hen instead of the normal 60. Though the results of this effort remained to be seen, Stephen continued to bubble with enthusiasm over his various projects to improve the conditions of the local farming community. He continued to hold institutes for them, to visit them in their homes and to raise demonstration plots to show how much more, and what better quality, could be raised on an acre of land.

My own work, too, was constantly on the increase, and the Chinese staff continued to grow. All of our nursing graduates who did not marry, and even some who had, joined in the work with interest and enthusiasm. Because it was thought that we should set up a medical center in Fourteenth Town, two nurses were sent there to live. I went there once a week to treat the difficult cases. Soon after, another center was set up in the like manner at White Cloud Ferry, so two nurses went there also. Since Dr. Dang still needed much rest, I had to run the two hospitals as well as make weekly calls to the two village dispensaries. In addition we maintained a program of periodic medical tours to the other villages. This meant starting at dawn every day and working right through until late at night. I slept wherever I was when the day was done.

Because chairs were so expensive, unreliable and slow, I usually walked to visit the remote villages. This meant aching feet from tortuous stone paths and steep climbs through the frightful Fukien heat during many months. I really needed a saddle pony. Somehow the local commander of the troops at the county seat heard how hard I was working and sent me a strong Mongolian pony. What a convenience! I had a servant ride him to Sixth Town because I had to drive in a load of kerosene and medicine. The next morning I left on my new pony on the long, dangerous, and difficult trip to tend the clinics at Fourteenth Town and White Cloud Ferry.

The soldiers had told me the pony did not know how to swim, but I had to cross the river in order to get to White Cloud Ferry. The boatmen did not know how deep the water was at the crossing, and naturally they did not want to risk loading a fractious pony into their little boat. So I sat in the boat and introduced that Mongolian pony to swimming by pulling his reins. He swam beautifully. At White Cloud Ferry that day I had to remove a tumor the size of a child's head from a buttock. Having already ridden eighteen miles to reach White Cloud Ferry, nine miles remained of that pony's trot before I would reach home. The pony arrived pulling at the bit, not sweating at all, but I could hardly get into the house. It was my first time on a horse in five years.

In December 1934, I was called to Foochow to see my good friend Mr. Sia who had become ill while there on a visit. I found him in serious condition with what looked like cerebral malaria. The Magaw laboratory report showed that his blood was packed with plasmodia. Yet, one doctor was treating him for typhoid, while another was sure his trouble stemmed from an infection in his feet. Mr. Sia was still mentally alert, but was unable to see or talk. His wife sat by him constantly while they poured saline into his veins and thus increased the cerebral pressure, already too high from blocked arterioles. As I saw it, small cerebral vessels were blocked with clumps of plasmodia.

His temperature climbed steadily and he died.

My good friend and pastor had always given me the right advice through so many perilous situations. Now this beautiful young man in the prime of life was gone, leaving behind a widow and five children. He also left behind parishes on both sides of the Min River where people would long remember his friendly attitude, his upright character, and his wise counsel.

Just before I left Foochow someone brought word that there had been a bad fire at the county seat. When the boat pulled in the next day, however, I was not prepared for what I saw. The town had become a wide expanse of smoking ashes, a great void of silence. The whole place had gone up in smoke, but as we rounded the last corner I discovered to my surprise that the little hospital was still standing. In the still-smoking ashes a couple of lonely pigs grunted disconsolately. All of the cloth shops, the vegetable, rice, and umbrella booths, even the post office no longer remained. I went to the hospital and heard all the details of the holocaust from Cung Dai. The fire had begun in the barber shop. It quickly spread, pushed by a vigorous wind, until the whole town was engulfed. People fled to the hills with what valuables and belongings they could carry. The hospital, church, and Boys' School had been saved only by a sudden change in the direction of the wind.

But even before the ashes were cold people had begun to pull together what remained. When I arrived at 5:00 A.M., already a small table stood in the midst of the warm ashes displaying a few seedy umbrellas for sale. Soon another small table appeared with a few oranges, and then another with vegetables. By breakfast time a makeshift meat counter had been started. Later in the morning a man had already put

Mintsing Jail

together a mud stove and a table; he was serving meals to standing customers. Gradually the inhabitants came back. In the afternoon the little city was again alive with people who began the hard work of setting up homes and businesses in the midst of ashes not yet cold. With this kind of spirit, I thought, China could never be vanquished.

I sensed a renewed thrill of wonder at the great potential these people possessed. They had centuries and centuries of high culture and profound spiritual concepts behind them, as well as magnificent historical achievements. I admired their strength and stamina. They were stubbornly loyal to what they believed; they suffered and even died for what they thought was right. I had great faith in their ability to grow and develop in new ways. I believed the Chinese would eventually build, perhaps when the United States had begun to decline, the greatest country in the world.

23
My Last Days in Mintsing

Now BACK in Mintsing in December 1934, a letter came from the bishop telling me to go home on furlough at once. Early in the summer I had gone to Magaw Hospital to have a troublesome molar removed. Since there was no dental surgeon, the task was undertaken by the general surgeon. It took him all morning and much of the afternoon to remove the tooth; in doing so, he cut not only the artery but also the nerve. Trismus developed from the hammering on my jaw, and I was unable to open my mouth through all the ensuing months. What food I was able to eat had to enter through space provided by an extracted incisor. I was very uncomfortable and now was not unhappy to return to the United States for special treatment before the jaw fibrosed.

But I was not willing to miss Christmas in Mintsing, so we went ahead with our plans. Moon Lily, Cung Dai, and I celebrated the occasion at the county seat. The most memorable event that day was our bringing a hot meal to prisoners in the local jail. Pastor Lau joined us, and we walked through the new street single file carrying the dinner. Pastor Lau brought a great basket of oranges. Another man carried two kerosene tins full of steaming hot noodles. Cung Dai's brother carried a great pot of cooked pork.

An official admitted us to a wooden-barred enclosure. Here we faced a second set of wooden bars. Behind the inner bars prisoners occupied very dark, vile-smelling damp rooms. A man emerged from the darkness, his face a green pallor and his body covered with scabies, with chains fastened to his ankles. I had wanted to bring a bar of soap for each prisoner, but was told not to bother since the prisoners were never allowed any water for washing. Another man came out of the shadows. His face was so ill, pathetic, and hopeless that I felt physically ill. These were human beings, but they were caged like beasts—in utter misery, hungry, cold, unclean. They suffered terrible emotional distress, with sentences of indefinite length. Many had left families penniless. Several men began to move slowly out of the shadows, chains clanking at every step. How their poor, red eyes brightened when they saw the savory hot noodles and delicious pork. Pastor Lau and Cung Dai ladled out the food into each bowl held through the bars. One prisoner was ashamed to show himself and had another man bring his bowl to be filled.

One of the prisoners was a broken old man who had been jailed because his son was a bandit. Another was a young boy in his teens, incarcerated for an indefinite period because a neighbor had reported that he "planned" to be a bandit. Another young man had been put in this filthy black hole to cure him of his opium habit. Another had been one of our young teachers who had left us to become a local law enforcement officer. He took his duties very seriously; all went well until he punished a rich man with a $1,000 fine. Now he was in jail for five years. Rich men knew how to pull strings. I wondered how long this wretched penal system would be tolerated. Surely it did nothing to rehabilitate the poor human beings who fell into its clutches.

Before leaving Mintsing I tried desperately to get permission from the Chinese government to take Hwa Sing with me. But it was not easy to take a Chinese girl out of the country, for there was a new law against it. Much against my will I was forced to leave her behind. Stephen agreed to take her in my absence. By this time my other daughter, Hwa Hui, was already at Hwa Nan College in Foochow.

Then I had to go through the heartbreaking farewell feasts and meetings. At the feasts, when it came time to make the expected speech, I told of my dreams for future service in Mintsing; there were so many more ways we could give service. Among other things, the two girls we had already sent to the mothercraft school would soon graduate. I hoped they would be appointed as teachers in the surrounding villages, subsidized by the hospital work, where they would impart some of their knowledge to the mothers of the area.

Then it was time to leave. My suitcases were put in the car. All the staff stood beside the car and presented me with gifts. I stood there in the rain crying like a fool under my umbrella. Then all the nurses were crying. Business Manager Wong ran off. The three boy nurses could not speak. Stephen's eyes were red.

Finally I regained enough composure to hand each servant some money wrapped in a red paper parcel. Then I got into the car and left, followed by an ear-splitting bombardment of firecrackers. Stephen and my two girls came with me down the Min River from Foochow to see me off on the boat to Shanghai. Hwa Sing was now old enough to know that this was a real parting. All the way downriver she crept inside my coat and sat perfectly still and silent. When I stepped up on to the steamer she begged to be taken aboard to see it, but when the whistle blew and I handed her down to Stephen, she fought and screamed to be allowed to go with me. I stood on deck sadly watching their little launch fade away upriver, back to Mintsing without me.

On the way to Shanghai I remembered the very last outcall that I had made before my departure. I was so ill with malaria at the time that I had to ride in a chair across the creek and up the steep mountain. The husband followed closely behind my chair and talked all the way up the stairs. "She has been in labor five days already," he told me.

"Why did you wait so long to call me?" I asked.

"We had not heard of you. We called the fortune tellers and drum beaters when the midwives all failed. Then a woman visiting in our village said that years ago she had lived in Sixth Town where there was a foreign woman who could deliver babies."

"Did you go to Sixth Town?" I asked.

"No, I thought first I would go to the county seat and inquire about this matter. Then someone told me you were there in that hospital."

The husband told me his wife was thirty years old. She had been married to another man when she was fourteen and had had two babies. After the second baby the husband's family decided to sell her to this man, a widower with three adult sons. This baby was the first of this new marriage. When we arrived the young wife was unconscious and very pale. Her pulse was barely perceptible. The husband began crying and went outside. With forceps I quickly delivered a beautiful baby boy. Outside the door the whole family was already chanting a death song. The young mother slowly regained consciousness. After some time I raised her head and put a cup of tea to her lips. The husband came in the room just then and found her drinking tea. Again he burst into tears and fell on his knees before me. Still weeping, he looked up at me and said, "When you go back to 'Beautiful Country' [the name in Chinese for the United States], please carry my thanks to the good people who sent out a doctor to help us in our hour of need."

I left a very happy couple with their big, baby boy and rode down the steep mountain side through fresh green pine and fir—sweetly fragrant, sturdy, and clean in the soft sunlight. Far below wound the wide, vividly blue creek, edged with white sand and dotted with tiny human figures who came and went on a miniature ferry. What a beautiful country. What a wonderful people!

24
Nanchang

I ARRIVED in Shanghai in June 1936, after more than a year away from China. There I was met by Cung Dai and Hwa Sing, now a young lady of seven. Together we boarded a train for Nanchang, capital of Kiangsi province, where I had agreed to work for a year before returning to Mintsing. Cung Dai sat beside me and told me of all that had transpired in Mintsing since I had left. Part of me ached to return to Mintsing and to the simple, hard life there; but the other half of me longed to see other parts of China with its great variety of customs, dialects, and people. I wanted to know more about China, and at that particular time I felt that returning to Mintsing would be too restrictive. Also, I wanted more experience in surgery. Then I would be ready to return to Mintsing.

We rode for two days, first southward into Chekiang province, and then westward into Kiangsi province, on a railroad that had been completed during my seventeen-month absence. It seemed to me that China had jumped ahead 100 years, and it was very thrilling for me to ride in such ease after all the years of difficult travel in boats, chairs, and on horseback. My old friend from Philadelphia days, Dr. Huang, and her staff welcomed us at the Nanchang station. Soon we were settled in a big mission residence.

Hwa Sing and I temporarily had to share our quarters with a missionary who was soon to leave on a furlough. This missionary refused to permit Hwa Sing to eat at our table because she was Chinese. Because this woman was soon to leave, I decided to accept the situation and not make trouble. My little girl therefore had her meals with Dr. Huang. I was wrong. I should not have accepted it for one meal. Keeping peace was not as important as registering the strongest possible protest against such racial discrimination. It sickened me that such people had come to China to "convert" the Chinese.

Dr. Huang filled me in on the history of this big hospital which I had now come to help her run. Many years before, Miss Gertrude Howe, a Methodist missionary in Kiukiang, had adopted and raised five Chinese girls. One of the five was Ida Kahn (K'ang Ch'eng), who became a doctor.* She had been practicing in Kiukiang for several years when in 1900 she was called to visit a patient in Nanchang. On this trip the doctor was accompanied by a woman missionary who failed to wear Chinese clothes and thus was very conspicuous. In Nanchang a mob, excited by the presence of a strange-looking foreigner, surrounded them and began throwing stones. Fortunately, the two women found shelter in the home of their patient before anyone was injured. But the Chinese woman doctor was so disturbed by this violent racial hatred she had witnessed that she asked the bishop to send her to Nanchang to begin medical work. In 1902 she settled in Nanchang with Miss Howe, her foster mother. Her medical work so impressed the local people that they gave her money to build a small clinic. She and Miss Howe used their own money to support the medical work. Finally, the local citizens felt such good will toward them that the city fathers contributed 1,000 piculs of rice from the public granary. With the proceeds from the sale of this rice the doctor bought land and built a good dispensary. Later the bishop was so delighted with her work and influence that he raised funds to build the splendid residence in which I now lived. In another few years she had received so many gifts from the

* A devout Methodist, K'ang Ch'eng (1873–1930?), with her close friend, Shih Mei-yü (Mary Stone), was one of China's first woman medical doctors. Having completed her medical training at the University of Michigan Medical School in 1896, she dedicated her life to bring modern medical services, religious education, and social welfare programs to the people of Central China.

local people that funds were sufficient to build a large hospital, which she had run by herself until Dr. Huang joined her after her year's stay with me in Mintsing. Dr. Ida Kahn had died a few years before my arrival, so Dr. Huang had been carrying a very heavy burden since that time with no other doctor to help.

Despite the terrific heat of the summer I began to explore this interesting, ancient Chinese city. Its name had been changed many times in various dynastic periods until finally it took its present name in the Ming dynasty, nearly 500 years before. It was said locally that the first city wall had been built around 200 B.C.—twenty-nine feet high, with six gates and surrounded by a fifteen-foot moat.

When General Chiang Kai-shek took Nanchang in 1927, he had the city wall torn down and the moat filled in. In its place was built a road named "Round-the-City-Horse-Road" which had a diameter of two miles. The street which led to the other mission compounds—the schools, church, and general hospital—was "Round-the-Lake-Road." I loved to travel on this road which bordered a lake that stood out like a beautiful jewel right in the heart of the city. This lake often appeared like a sheet of pure silver, with white mists hanging like fairies over its smooth surface. Wild ducks, in soft gray, or black and white, swam silently over the clear water. Around the edges of the lake appeared splashes of pure white and rust red, the reflections of homes that lined the shore. A small island stood in the middle of the lake. Sometimes a lavender haze covered the lake in the late afternoon, but the colors of the lake were so variable that one would have to pass it for years to know its full repertoire. Across the street from the lake was a great public park, rich with gorgeous flowers and supplied with wading pools for little children, modern-style exercise bars and slides, a ball park, and a band stand and free movies for all.

But that was the modern part of the city. There was another area which had been largely undisturbed by progress. I loved to roam there. The streets were wide enough for only one ricksha. These streets were paved with hand-cut stones, each about three feet in length and hollowed by centuries of passing feet. Here were the old-time stalls, their fronts open to the street, where all sorts of articles could be bought. In this section the historic Bridge of the Lofty Scholars, in pure white marble, arched a little stream. Women could be seen clinging to the beautifully carved marble posts while they prayed for babies. The old examination stalls of the Ch'ing dynasty were said to have been near this bridge, but I saw no trace of them.

Getting to know Nanchang—seeing the Pagoda of the Golden Cord, the public kitchens where rice was given to the needy, the orphanages—came on my afternoons off. The rest of my time was spent in the big compound or making sick calls. When we arrived in June the compound was fragrant with gardenias, *lan-hwa,* and magnolias, all in full bloom. The *lan-hwa* was a rare orchid, a bell-shaped, pale-green flower spotted with brown. They gave off a heavenly perfume. The scent of the compound's great magnolia trees, full of waxen white flowers, made me almost delirious. I loved to look out at night to see the blossoms glowing white in the darkness.

In this setting Hwa Sing and I lived together with a local woman to cook and clean for us. One afternoon, late in July, Hwa Sing suddenly uttered a shriek and tore out the door. She had heard someone speaking Fukienese. I too rushed out and found Third Sister-in-law, who had taken care of Hwa Sing since she was a month old. She had come to join us from Fukien with Kai Cio, one of the male nurses from Sixth Town hospital. He had now come to work in Nanchang's general hospital. Hwa Hui, who was continuing her course in nursing at another hospital in Nanchang, joined us for a wonderful evening of Fukienese dialect and news from Mintsing. Mandarin was a new dialect for me, so this evening of Fukienese seemed like a real homecoming.

Summer passed. When September came, with the feel of autumn in the air, I thought constantly of Mintsing. I could see its valley of golden rice; the Prussian-blue river winding through the fields; the blue-clad men and women bringing in the harvest. I could smell the fragrance of the ripening rice heads. I could hear the thump of rice stalks as they were whacked against the receiving box. I could see the high mountains encircling this scene—blue against the gold, with little winding paths twisting and turning on their slopes off into the distant purple. I saw and smelled and heard harvest time in Mintsing. And my heart yearned for it. Little did I suspect then that I would never be able to return.

25

Patients in Kiangsi

NOVEMBER 1936, came with its glorious chrysanthemums and gorgeous dahlias. The Chinese have always admired the chrysanthemum. It is perhaps mentioned in their poems more frequently than any other flower. It is a "clean flower," a flower with "proud bones," like the scholars who raised them. They served as the symbol of long life and rugged endurance.

One of my first patients that month was a young woman whose abdomen was greatly distended as a result of an ovarian cyst. I did the operation with a local anesthesia, injecting Novocain along the line of the incision. The patient suffered no pain or discomfort and the fifteen-pound cyst was removed with no trouble.

Some weeks later we discovered an advertisement in the local Nanchang newspaper, which, translated literally, was as follows: "Thanks [to] Woman's and Children's Hospital. [I] received much. I, poor man Chiang Lok Sang. Wife, because abdomen strangely big, asked [doctor to] open knife. Doing that they took out a fifteen-pound thing shaped like a globe. In four weeks [she] left hospital, health normal. No way to express thanks except [in] newspaper. Chiang Lok Sang."

The news spread fast that there was a doctor at the hospital who "opened the knife." People came in increasing numbers. Two women with cancer of the breast came and I did a radical removal on both. Two came with tuberculosis of the spine and were greatly relieved when they were put on Bradford frames. We treated many, many pale children who were heavily infected with flukes. One little baby of eleven months had run a fever for months. One doctor had even opened his eardrums. We found plasmodia in his blood and treated him for malaria. In four days his fever was gone and he began to eat with a hearty appetite. According to medical books malaria causes a low white corpuscle count, but I found that in this case, as in many other cases in Mintsing, the white counts sometimes ran higher than normal.

One day a farmer and his wife brought in a very sick baby girl. "We have had nine children before this one; each one died of the same symptoms," the father said. I looked into the baby's throat and quickly gave her diphtheria antitoxin. Then I took a culture from the mother's throat. Since this was positive, the mother too was given the antitoxin until the cultures were negative. Meanwhile the baby recovered and the parents were ecstatic.

"The mother had tiny worms in her throat," I explained to the father. "So I gave her the needles to kill the worms. Now you can take your baby home and rest your heart that she is well."

A beggar woman brought in her little son who was almost dead. She had starved him viciously in order to enhance the appearance of her misery and thus improve her income. The baby was still alive, so we took him into the hospital. A week later he opened his eyes and stretched out a thin little hand. Now the mother wanted to take him out of the hospital. "If he gets well, he will spoil my business," she explained.

Since I could not change her mind, I called Miss Liu Tai-ching, our new social service worker, and told her the story.

She turned to the beggar woman and made her eyes very big. "If you take that baby home I shall report you to the police," she said sternly. The woman left hurriedly and we kept the boy until he was well.

One Sunday morning a man came to take me to his village. "My wife has been in labor for eight days," he explained. "No one can deliver her. Will the doctor come?" There was no highway to the village.

The only route was a stone-paved path which wound through seven miles of fields. The only conveyance was a Chinese-style wheelbarrow, with a high strong wheel at the center of the load. For passengers, this wheel was boxed in by a narrow shelf on each side. The nurse sat on one shelf and I on the other, our backs straight and feet braced against a footboard. A wide strap crossed over the shoulders of the wheelbarrow man, with the ends attached to each arm of his vehicle to help him balance the load. The wheel was made of a solid piece of thin wood, circled with an iron rim. It creaked in a very special way so that people far ahead could tell we were coming. The pavement of long narrow stones set end to end made the wheelbarrow bump dreadfully as it moved from one stone to the next in an almost hypnotic, monotonous rhythm. I would rather have walked, but that would have upset the balance and forced the nurse to walk. It took two hours to cover the seven miles.

As we approached the little village, its houses huddled close together, we could hear the thumping sound of looms busy at work and the barking of dogs. When we reached our destination we were not taken into the house, but rather into a very dirty shed. This shed was filled with men, women, and children who were yelling frightfully, beating drums and shaking long sticks with iron prongs on the ends. They were working hard to scare the devils away, but at the same time they were filling the already filthy shed with more dust. It was a horrible racket. The pregnant woman lay on the earth floor on a little pile of straw. A few women relatives squatted around her, tears streaming down their cheeks, as they moaned and wept as if in terrible agony. A fish net hung over this small group to prevent the devils from reaching the woman in labor.

The whole group paused momentarily in surprise at seeing the female foreign devil, with white skin and high nose, come walking in. I said to them, "Men and children will please leave the room while I deliver her." No one moved. Laughing, I seized one of the "devil forks" and began to shoo them out. Their first expressions of great alarm slowly melted into laughter as I kept smiling broadly. They all rushed out, the woman foreign devil still after them wielding the devil fork. Once out, they all rushed back in again, but finally the nurse and I got them all out. We barricaded the doors and windows with bags of rice. While the nurse boiled water and sterilized the instruments, I got the poor woman to lay down on a long grain box. Then, to the utter amazement of the women who all remained to watch, I delivered the baby with forceps. A big red disc of sun was just setting behind purple hills when everything was done; the woman was in good condition. We climbed back onto the wheelbarrow and bumped our way back to Nanchang. All along the road people stood in their doorways, just as they did in Mintsing, and as we passed they called out to the wheelbarrow man and other men who accompanied us. "Did she deliver the baby?"

The wheelbarrow man, or the man who carried the baskets of instruments, would yell out, "She pulled it out with long tongs!"

We heard people all along the route exclaim, "Truly, that woman is a living Buddha."

On another day I was called to East County, a small town eighty miles east of Nanchang. Since a railroad went right by the village, I went third-class on the Shanghai Express. The train stopped at many little stations. These stations were surrounded by high picket fences or barbed wire to keep local venders from pushing in too near the train. Country women, with black cloths over their heads, meekly held baskets of oranges, eggs, and six-inch lengths of sugar cane through the fences to passengers who ran over quickly to buy before the train resumed its journey. Little children thrust their cold hands through the fences, noisily exhibiting the wares that had previously been arranged by their parents. A few enterprising young men importantly shouldered others aside as they offered bamboo baskets of steamed dumplings wrapped in dirty cloths.

The houses in these villages were windowless mud structures with tiled roofs. They were built tightly together to make very compact communities. Ducks trailed along the new road that skirted the railroad. Pigs rode to market upside-down on Chinese wheelbarrows, one pig on each side of the center wheel and each trying to outsqueal his fellow sufferer, and the wheel as well. As the train slowly chugged along through fields of winter wheat, cabbage, turnips, and carrots, a cold gray sky—pierced here and there with glints of gold—brooded over distant hills.

At last the train pulled into East County where I was met by a tall, stout German missionary. He led me along a path between bare paddy fields to a village of 1,100 families. The village was surrounded by a very deep moat, twenty feet across, with high earthworks around its inner bank. A wall of bricks was being built to replace the earthen barricade. I asked if the village had been attacked by the communists three years before. It had been, but the army was on the run and had hurried on by without harming many people. The German missionary told me that many of the people in the village and area were in fairly comfortable circumstances. The farms outside the village were spacious and fertile and the town produced and exported tung oil as well as cane sugar, which was sold in wooden buckets.

We finally arrived at the German missionary's clean home. His wife constantly scolded her cook with no apparent regard for his feelings or understanding of the Chinese way of face saving. Their two-year-old daughter had had a fever of over 104 for six days. On examination I concluded the child was suffering from meningitis and had to be moved to the hospital. Since no train would come till the next day I spent the night in this missionary home and began to see something of their problem in adjusting to life in China. After two years neither spoke Chinese very well, and they appeared to consider their German ways of doing and thinking as the only legitimate course. They seemed lost, quite unable to adjust to life in an alien environment. I felt sorry for them, but also wondered what possible contribution such people could make to China.

We were able to cure the German couple's beautiful little daughter, and we sent her home. Some weeks later the father called me to his home again. Now the little girl was very ill with smallpox. "In my family we do not take vaccinations," the father said proudly. "For God takes care of us and we trust in Him."

A few days later his golden-haired child died in our hospital in Nanchang. After the funeral I took the two of them aside and said to them, "You lost your lovely little girl because you refused God's gift to her, the gift of vaccination. If you still refuse what God offers for the protection of your children, you may lose your baby boy also."

The parents then permitted me to vaccinate the baby boy. The Chinese lost many children because of an ignorance that could be understood. The ignorance of this German family I was unable to comprehend.

As winter descended in 1936, I began to enlarge the scope of our work. Through Miss Liu, the social service worker, we secured permission to visit the local prison for women, where eighty-five prisoners were confined. We found them packed into their nine bedrooms for the night. They were allowed only two barrels of water a day for drinking, washing, and cooking. Though they were supposed to be taught some sort of industrial work, they actually were idle all day long. The New Life Movement, sponsored by the Nationalist government, had done nothing for this group.

The women prisoners crowded eagerly around us. Each was anxious to tell us about her ailments. The wife of the communist who beheaded Mr. and Mrs. Stams a few years before was one of the prisoners; we treated her for trachoma. This unfortunate woman was only twenty-seven years old, but people said she had no hope ever to get out of prison; she had been with her husband and was party to the murders. No one would dare ask that her sentence be commuted. Another young girl had been sentenced for life because she had thrown her baby into the river. I recalled the practice I had observed to my horror in Fukien, where people threw their babies to the pigs or into the river with little apparent remorse. Miss Liu came with me every Sunday to the prison to talk to the women while I treated them.

On Easter Sunday I took each woman prisoner an Easter lily. The women had been standing at the barred gate waiting for us. When they saw the flowers they fought madly with each other to get their arms through the bars to reach for a flower. This desire for a flower, the love for something of beauty, convinced me that even these poor women possessed a wonderful potential if only it could be brought out. Miss Liu, with her high ideals and intelligent, sympathetic approach, seemed like just the right kind of person to make friends and win them over to better attitudes.

26

Chinese Orphanages, and Nanchang's Celebration of Chiang Kai-shek's Release (December 1936)

MISS LIU TAI-CHING was born in Hankow. When she was still a baby her father consented to have her engaged to the little son of a friend. But the boy was frail and often ill. He died just before their wedding day. Miss Liu went to her father after the funeral and asked him not to arrange another marriage. Because of her engagement, she believed it was her duty to take care of the deceased boy's mother as long as she lived. So she asked her father for permission to give her life to public service of some kind. Her father agreed, so she went to a school in Hankow for training in social service; later she worked in the Hankow Y.W.C.A. for a number of years. She had been appointed to Nanchang just before I arrived. Her first move on coming to Nanchang had been to organize the educated and privileged women of the city. She told them what they could do to help deal with some of the social problems that afflicted the city. The result of her program of educating these women to the city's needs was the formation of the Nanchang Christian Women's Union, which provided the resources for her various projects.

Miss Liu was a very intelligent yet warm person; she was clear in her thinking and upright in her character. She was completely absorbed in people and their problems. We became very good friends. Very soon after my arrival, Miss Liu took me to the City Orphanage on Chopstick Street. It was a very large old Chinese house, painted red with green window casings, with dark rooms and cool courts. We entered a large room. It was filled with rows of bamboo baskets set on rockers; each basket contained two small babies. This politically controlled refuge for unwanted babies had a death rate of over 100 infants per month. One day 40 died. There had been only one old crone to serve as wet nurse for each 3 babies. One wash cloth and basin had been used for all of the babies. Consequently gonorrhea had traveled like wildfire through the institution and a large percentage of the babies were blind.

Recently, however, a fine young woman, trained for this work in Peiping, had been engaged to improve the facilities and services. The Women's Christian Union strongly supported her for the coming battle against those who had profited from the institution's mismanagement. Gradually this hard-working woman brought intelligent young girls to work in the orphanage and trained them to give formulas and good care to the babies. A washcloth and basin was obtained for each baby. In the next few months this caused the number of infected eyes to be reduced remarkably, and the death rate dropped to eighteen to twenty per month. Furthermore, the new director was successful in finding good homes for the babies. In Nanchang many women wanted to adopt either daughters or daughters-in-law to raise for their sons; but they had to be healthy babies.

Miss Liu also took me to see a home for orphans between eight and fourteen years old. These 250 boys and girls were the sturdy children of hard-working farmers in southern Kiangsi. Their parents had loved and cared for them. We were told that when the communists arrived to set up an independent government, their policy had been to kill the adults in order to indoctrinate the children. Whether or not this story was true, we did know that in the course of the fighting hordes of men and boys had been killed, as had large numbers of women. Some of the missionaries who had been in that part of the province thought that a million people had perished as a result of the communist occupation of the area and the government's effort to extricate them.

In the early 1930s Chiang Kai-shek had sent armies into Kiangsi to wipe out the communists. Not only the terrific fighting, but also the army's scorched-earth policy had meant death by starvation for thousands of peasants. When the communist forces fled in 1934 on their historic 6,000-mile trek to the west and north, they left behind thousands of orphans who were too young to make the march. Each group of orphans now lived in an old home or in a temple, where the only furniture was a cot apiece.

At Christmas time, 1936, Miss Liu took me to another such orphanage which was home for 160 children. We all stood in a courtyard of the old temple for a Christmas program. Miss Liu's youngest adopted daughter and Hwa Sing sang Christmas songs for the children. Then Miss Liu asked the orphan children to sing something. The 160 children stood together, threw back their heads, and sang with great volume in perfect rhythm and harmony; their beautiful faces glowed with pleasure. It touched me to tears to watch those brave youngsters who had lived through such terror. They were strong and healthy, and apparently happy. They would make fine citizens for China when they grew up. I thought that all of their suffering had helped to develop and mature them.

Shortly after this I joined a group, led by a high-ranking official's wife, to take a hot meal to another orphanage just outside the city. When the group entered the institution and looked at the expectant faces, we were all moved. Then the high-ranking lady began her flowery presentation speech; but suddenly she could no longer speak because she was so overcome by emotion. Tears streamed down her cheeks. Then the children began to cry. All of us wept.

That evening our hospital gave a big feast for the staff, teachers, and pastors of the city. Just before the guests arrived I received a letter from the new mayor of Mintsing, urging me to return to my old work and promising government backing. Indeed, I dreamed of returning to that lonely spot to put my shoulder again to the task of easing Mintsing's burden of disease, superstition, and illiteracy. My heart ached to go.

Dr. Huang, a man in charge of the big provincial hospital in Nanchang, sat beside me at the feast that night. We talked about projects to improve medical care in China. "Where were you before coming here?" he asked.

I told him of my work in Mintsing.

"No good doctor should go out into rural work," he said. "The government policy is to train second-rate people to go to such places. They can take care of all they are trained to deal with and ship to the city what cases they are unequipped to handle. It will take China 50 to 100 years to train enough doctors to take care of all our people. Meanwhile, every full-fledged doctor should work in a city center."

Then we talked of General Chiang Kai-shek, who had been kidnapped in Sian by Chang Hsüeh-liang at the instigation of the communists.* No one could predict the outcome. Then someone hurried into the room and announced excitedly, "The General has been freed!"

"A false alarm," said someone, and they all went on eating. Dr. Huang and I slipped from our seats and went out onto the veranda. There we could hear the uproar of the excited city. Crowds were yelling and singing, firecrackers were booming constantly.

* Chiang Kai-shek had consistently argued, even in face of Japanese aggression after 1931, that the Japanese were a disease of the skin while the Chinese communists were a disease of the flesh. After the communists gathered at Yenan, Shensi, in 1935 following their historic Long March from Kiangsi to the Northwest, Chiang sought to administer the coup de grâce. He ordered the "Young Marshall" Chang Hsüeh-liang's Manchurian army to attack. Faced with a growing sentiment among the troops and their commanders that they should fight the Japanese rather than the communists, Chiang flew to Sian on December 3, 1936, to exhort his men. On December 12, a mutiny occurred; Chiang was "kidnapped" and forced to accept a second United Front with the communists in order to resist Japan. He returned to Nanking on Christmas day, a national hero.

Official word now came that Madame Chiang had flown to Sian to help obtain the release of her husband. Later we were told that the communists took Chiang's pocket notebook and found not one selfish thought in the entire book. Every page was filled with ideas to improve his country. In any case, it was very politic to let Chiang free; such a gesture would surely give them prestige. Outside our windows the whole city seemed to have gone mad with joy; far into the night people shouted and sang and set off firecrackers. The next day the streets and parks were jammed with people still wild with happiness. Newspapers reported the same reaction all over China.

On Christmas Eve the city held a mammoth parade in honor of Chiang's release. Enormous red and yellow paper lanterns were carried in a very long procession. Some were shaped like airplanes; others were formed in the shape of great gates, with Chiang's name written at the top. Some represented various political leaders, and I could make out the resemblance to Chiang Kai-shek, Chang Hsüeh-liang, and other famous officials. The city buses were magnificently trimmed for the parade with a full-length portrait of Chiang on the front of each. The passengers in these buses were various city leaders.

Every kind of Chinese musical instrument was brought to the parade. Countless poles of firecrackers boomed continuously. The singing, shouting, cheering, music, and thundering fireworks filled everyone with excitement. Hundreds of men carried lighted torches. The parade was two miles long. As it wound along Round-the-Lake-Road, I looked at the reflections of its red and golden lights in the still waters of the lake, while the music, the shouting, and the rumbling firecrackers gradually faded away into the distance.

27
High Hopes for the New Life Movement and Change

AFTER CHRISTMAS 1936, I became interested in the New Life Movement, which the Nationalist government now sponsored. Occasionally I met with Dora Wong, the new chairman of the Woman's Department of the New Life Movement. She was a charming and intelligent woman who was dedicated to her work. This movement had been launched to promote the old Confucian standards of *I* (regulated attitudes), *Li* (right conduct), *Lien* (honesty), and *Ch'ih* (integrity). The basic idea behind the movement was to reform the Chinese people, to build a sound economy and to sponsor the rebirth of the Chinese nation.

Dr. Huang and Miss Liu took me to my first New Life Movement meeting. This was a woman's meeting. It was held in a big auditorium and policed by chubby young girls in police uniforms who zealously evicted squalling babies and their mothers from the audience. This was something unusual, to be sure, for everywhere I had been in China crying babies were tolerated. In Mintsing, for example, no one minded babies holding forth during a church service. The meeting's general theme was that everyone should do work with her hands. The speaker told us that it was an old-fashioned idea that it was undignified for those with money or position to work. She went on to say that it was wrong for any student to be exempted from work. She argued that study was indeed necessary but that it should not go unbalanced with manual labor. In my opinion, if this idea could be accepted by Chinese intellectuals, it would be another big step forward in the formation of a new China. The room displayed a fine exhibit of handwork, mostly sewing and embroidery, which was designed to impress the visitors to go home and also learn to make such things.

On the way home I asked more about this new movement. Dr. Huang and Miss Liu told me that, among other things, the goals were clean living, elimination of extravagance, elimination of squeeze and graft, and the prohibition of smoking and spitting in public. The movement aimed to raise the standard of living of the Chinese and create a new society. The leaders of the movement hoped to prepare the Chinese people to move from an agricultural way of life to that of an industrialized state. The New Life Movement was thus conceived of as one element in China's effort to modernize. The need had long been recognized, and now the government began to promote projects to develop natural resources, improve agricultural production, establish new industries, and improve transportation and river conservation. Taxation would have to be put on a scientific basis, and cooperation between capital and labor had to be achieved.

One immediate effect of the movement could already be seen in the more courteous conduct of the police, conductors, and other public servants.

"Trains go on schedule now," one remarked proudly.

"And they are clean," added another.

"Smoking and spitting are not allowed now anywhere on Nanchang streets."

"No one can go around with buttons unbuttoned."

The new ethic also applied to foreigners. One of the men missionaries in Nanchang was politely approached by a policeman who asked him to button all the buttons on his overcoat.

Dr. Huang and Miss Liu told me of a team of seventeen university students. These students were living in a temple in south Kiangsi trying to rehabilitate the area after the tragedy of civil war. These were courageous young people who willingly risked their health to enter that malaria-afflicted, poverty-stricken area where there was very little to eat. I was also told about the "hundreds of thousands" of volunteers who were being trained in a rigorous three-month program to work in anticommunist crusades. One of their goals was to keep salt, food, and cotton from entering the communist-held territory surrounding Yenan, the new communist capital in Shensi. Most of these were student volunteers, whose own friends were not to know what they were doing. Each volunteer was paid $12 per month. This money, I was told, came partly from the Boxer Indemnity fund and partly from the provincial and central governments. Other volunteers were being trained to supervise the postal system; to assist the army, and to see that the common people were being treated fairly.

After completing the training program each group went out to train local people in various localities. The aim was to put leadership into the hands of local people as much as possible. In their local bases, they set up compulsory schools for children between seven and ten for four months. The best of these pupils were then appointed as teachers for the next four-month course for beginners. Rudimentary medical centers were also established. In addition, the volunteers were to help settle disputes, encourage road-building, rehabilitate prostitutes, eliminate gambling and opium-smoking, loan money, feed refugees, and help farmers. I wondered how much of such an ambitious program could be put into practice immediately, but at the time it was very exciting to see that people were beginning to sense the need for real reform. My informants told me that these volunteer groups were also actively engaged in encouraging economy in weddings, setting up libraries and public clocks, establishing efficient fire-fighting teams, and supporting shelters and dormitories for coolies and beggars.

In the year before I arrived in Nanchang, fifty-seven New Life Movement centers had been established in China. People said it was spreading like wildfire. It seemed to many of us foreigners that China had begun to settle down from its costly and murderous civil wars to work for reconstruction on a vast scale.

While in Nanchang I had the opportunity to meet many Chinese leaders. One of these was Mr. Chang Fu-liang, Chairman of the National Economic Council. This man was very active in reconstruction work. The League of Nations had sent three experts to suggest means to deal with the shocking conditions of south Kiangsi. The team recommended that $1,900,000 be set aside from the Wheat and Cotton Loan, and that this amount be used to support cooperatives, to establish an agricultural institute and rural welfare centers, and to improve public health and rural schools. Mr. Chang was in charge of the program. Centers were chosen close to a road or railway. Temples or other public buildings were used to house the project offices. Intelligent local people were being trained for leadership responsibilities, and in each center the program sponsored agricultural, educational, and health work; in addition, agricultural cooperatives were established. One of the primary economic programs called for reforestation, especially of the area's tung trees —the oil of which could be exported—as well as of wax trees, pine and fruit trees. The program also sought to improve strains of rice, geese, and pigs. Something was beginning to be done to control insects that damaged large portions of the crops.

The program planned to set up a school for each 100 families in the area to offer primary education and some vocational courses. On paper at least, the plan was to add 4,000 schools per year until the goal was attained. The program envisioned cooperatives to transport crops, improve sugar cane refining, and revive native industries such as tea, linen, and porcelain production. Health work was to be centralized and rationalized. The new Provincial Hospital in Nanchang, headed by Dr. Huang, cousin of my close friend, Dr. Yen-yü Huang, would care for the serious cases which were to be sent in from all over the province. Each rural health center was supposed to have a doctor, a nurse, and midwife, but it was impossible to find a doctor for each center. The program recognized the need to provide vaccinations for the vast population. Mute testimony to this urgent need was the presence of fifty altars to the goddess of smallpox within a radius of three miles.

One afternoon Miss Liu took me to see the government-supported Common People's Industrial Homes. This project housed poor families. The homes were small brick structures. The yards were clean; the whitewashed rooms had board floors. Each house had an apartment for two families, consisting of a single bedroom for each family and a common living room and kitchen. In one of these homes I met Mrs. Chiang Lok-sang, the removal of whose cyst had been advertised in a Nanchang newspaper. She seemed very pleased to see me. As we sipped tea I asked what her husband did.

"He is a tea boy in the government school. His pay is $12.00 a month."

"Does the school give him meals?" I asked.

"They deduct $3.50 from his salary for his meals," she explained.

"Do you have to pay rent?" I asked.

"Yes, we pay $3.00 a month rent. That leaves $5.50 for food and clothes for me and our five children."

We visited the teaching center for this project and watched women who were learning how to weave; the men were being taught to make baskets.

Another local leader I met was Mr. Huang, Commissioner of Police. Three of us were invited by him to dinner at the smart Burlington Hotel, where we had an American meal of squab and ice cream. It was a fascinating evening. Many other Americans were dining there that evening—men in the motion picture business, explorers, writers, and businessmen. Mr. Huang told us he had 2,000 police under his jurisdiction. His department cost the government $20,000 per month. His police all dressed in smart uniforms, black leather shoes, white gaiters, white gloves, and helmets. The city was so safe that a woman could walk on the streets at night without fear. I asked Mr. Huang if he thought China was overpopulated.

"No, it has food enough to feed all its people. The problem is transportation. We need to be able to quickly and efficiently move food from a productive province to one suffering from famine or floods. Our transportation needs developing."

Postal Commissioner Liu also entertained us in his home. He was a very pleasant man, with a gracious wife and seven beautiful, courteous children. We ate an exquisite Chinese meal, surrounded by four electric fans. I asked him about Chiang Kai-shek.

"He is a wonderful man and is doing so much for his people with his whole heart," Mr. Liu said. "But we are very troubled about conditions now. The communists are getting stronger in the north, the Japanese are threatening our east, and some of our countrymen are planning an uprising in the south."

One evening the wealthy father of one of our young nurses invited me to dinner with a group of prosperous businessmen. My host had been with Standard Oil for thirty years. I told of my admiration for the progressive programs under way in Nanchang and other parts of China, as well as for the goals of the New Life Movement. Then my Chinese host led the conversation around to religion. "I am afraid I am not too orthodox," I said.

He mentioned the Oxford Groups which had spread over much of China's larger centers, and which I had met in Foochow. I told him what little I knew about it, and mentioned the points that I thought valuable in its teachings.

"Chiang Kai-shek has been living along those lines for six months," he said.

"He is a man of very noble character," said a Chinese guest. "He is in a very difficult position, facing many serious problems. But he begins each day at 4:00 A.M. with a time of quiet, a prayer, a meditation."

"His influence is working all over the nation," said another. "Many of his public officials have become Christians."

I also began to meet other Westerners in Nanchang. Willo Marie Hecker, a missionary nurse at the General Hospital, became very friendly with me. Her interest in medical work, her absence of racial discrimination, and her sense of humor made her the best of companions for the adventures we shared in China. On one occasion we met two young American men who taught at Yale-in-China in Changsha. The young American teachers were interested in Chinese life, history, and art; this endeared them to both of us. They wanted to see all aspects of Chinese life, and they spent some of their summer vacation making trips on donkeys into the back country. We had a delightful day together. The four of us visited the leper colony south of Nanchang. This was a well-built institution, pleasantly situated. A male nurse resided there and gave shots regularly to the patients. No shocking lesions were to be seen (in contrast to what I had seen in Mintsing); unlike the colony in Mintsing, there was not an atmosphere of hopelessness. The patients evidenced apathy, a symptom of the disease, but they were disciplined and cared for. They all worked daily in a large garden in the colony.

People from all over the world had come to Nanchang. We met Mr. Caffarena, who worked in the Salt Revenue Administration; Mrs. Caffarena was a charming aristocratic woman whose English was infinitely better than my French. We enjoyed many conversations together. The Caffarenas had discovered over 200 Chinese in Nanchang who spoke French, so they often held an open house for them. Willo and I sometimes played tennis with their daughter and Dr. Riego, a Filipino doctor from the General Hospital. The tennis courts were located at the Officer's Moral Endeavor Union, which occupied a splendid site high on a hill overlooking the Kan River. It was a fascinating life.

28

Medicine, a Car, and a New-Style Wedding

SPRING 1937, came in March. The grass suddenly turned green and the big Nanchang compound was transformed. Birds sang vociferously, and the wonderful old magnolias came into full bloom—along with purple violets, forsythias, daffodils and strawberry blossoms. The golden *mei-hua* blossoms perched like gay butterflies over the lovely shrubs, the roses appeared in all colors, and scents and the narcissus began to open.

That spring we saw more and more cases in the hospital. Some were unusual and interesting. A six-month-old baby girl was brought in suffering from a birth defect. Her bowel movements came through the vagina. I successfully opened up the intestine and repaired the lesion in the vagina. Very soon afterwards two more children who suffered the same defect were brought in, and again the operations were successful.

A woman appeared one day with a very large ovarian cyst. When I operated I found that the mesentery* had adhered to the whole front portion of the great cyst. This entailed a very long and tedious job of cutting and tying countless large blood vessels. The appendix was also glued to the cyst, so that too had to be dissected out. When we finally lifted out the big cyst, we put it on the scales; it weighed exactly 40 pounds. I made the incision under local anesthesia and then gave Nembutal intravenously. The patient slept peacefully throughout.

In addition to such duties as were provided me by the hospital, by the spring I had begun some local health programs. Dr. Huang had agreed to support two nurses in such work, so we began to concentrate on preventive health measures in some of the local schools. Also, we began to do follow-up work on the hospital patients, visiting each one in his own home and offering health information to meet particular requirements. We also began evening classes for the cooks, amahs,† and other servants of the hospital. Miss Liu and I also started baby clinics. The mothers and babies met on our beautiful lawns, where Miss Liu taught them songs, told stories, directed games, and discussed child care. Before leaving, each mother brought her child to me for a free medical examination. Appeals had also come from villages outside Nanchang for me to set up clinics. I thought that if I could buy a small car, this might indeed be practicable. As in Mintsing, such clinics could be run by nurses, and I would visit them once each week.

That spring I also attended the provincial medical convention which was held at the Provincial Hospital. Forty doctors came to the meeting; only four were women. I was the only American. It was a very pleasant experience for me, even though I was unable to understand all of what was said in the lectures. My Mandarin was not yet very proficient. Then, at the end of March, I took the train (third class) to Shanghai to attend the national medical convention. Peach and plumb

* Folds that connect the intestines to the abdominal wall.

† A wet nurse or maidservant in charge of children.

trees were in full bloom all the way through Chekiang. As we approached Hangchow the fields of blossoming rape appeared to be rich carpets of gold. A thousand doctors attended the meeting and again I found it very stimulating. The papers were delivered in Mandarin, English, and German.

While in Shanghai I bought a small Ford to drive to the village clinics we would set up in Kiangsi. Willo, who had come to Shanghai for medical treatment, was ready to return to Nanchang, so she accompanied me by car. Luckily, the Ford Motor Company lent us a chauffeur for the journey. We left Shanghai and drove directly south, the deep blue Pacific on our left while on the right the golden rape fields stretched away to purple mountains. That night we stayed at the famous ancient capital of Hangchow. Early the next morning we left the beautiful city and turned west. We traveled now over a fine surfaced road, a mirror-clear river on our left. White herons stood knee-deep in the water. Now and then we saw a loon dive as we approached. The nearby mountains were covered with a shrub that resembled a bridal wreath; the white of this shrub intermingled with masses of red azaleas in full bloom. Purple wistaria hung from tree tops; catalpas were in full bloom. Along the 560-mile trip we reveled at the beautiful old, wide-spreading camphors, the dainty groves of bamboos, the pines and the orchards of orange trees and mulberries. The winter wheat was still in the ground in many places, while a patch of tobacco appeared from time to time. Some farmers had harvested their wheat and were breaking ground for the spring rice; a few already were sowing the yellow rice kernels in the flooded paddies. At dusk we crossed the Chekiang border and entered Kiangsi province. When we arrived at Pearl City we entered through an outer and an inner gate, driving up a street so narrow our car could barely get through. Here we found an inn and spent the night.

The day before we had crossed rivers on ferries. But in Kiangsi we encountered high bridges over the streams. And such bridges! They had only one plank on each side for the wheels, but since they were set for ordinary-sized cars, the small Ford had a difficult time keeping its wheels on the planks. One bridge was fifty feet above a deep stream. If the chauffeur had not been driving I would have turned around and gone back to Shanghai. Even so, we broke two springs crossing those dreadful bridges.

In Chekiang we had noticed that the women wore skirts and a particular sort of head gear. Their dignified-looking houses were decorated in black and white. Their graves were decorated with willow branches which were trimmed with red paper. But as we now moved westward into Kiangsi, we found that the women wore trousers, that the houses were for the most part simple and unpainted with thatched roofs; on the graves red paper was simply held down with stones. The names of the hamlets, villages, and towns that we passed on the way were interesting to us. There was "Oil Tree Cottage," "Willow Village," "White Sands," "Arrow Quiver," "Swimming Dragon," "River Mouth," "Darting Sunbeams," "Precious Mountain Stream," "Eagle Pool," "Superabundant River," and "Eastern County," to name but a few.

In one such town we stopped for tea. Women gathered around us and asked the usual polite questions. "How old are you?" they asked Willo.

"Forty," she replied.

"Forty!" they shouted. "No such thing. You are not a day over twenty."

Then they looked at me and pondered. "That one is not a day over thirty," they said to each other. And then they asked me.

Along came an elderly man and they called out to him, "These two women say they are forty years old."

"Forty years old!" he laughed. Then he pulled a girl of about thirteen out from behind a door. "This one is fifty," he cackled and went his way muttering, "They say they are forty years old."

Early in the summer, after our return to Nanchang, we celebrated Beautiful Snow's marriage. Beautiful Snow had been one of our nurses at Mintsing. Her father had engaged her in infancy to the son of a fortune teller, but when she came to the Sixth Town hospital to study nursing she became acquainted with Able Strength, one of the male nurses. They fell in love and together saved enough money to buy off the fortune teller. But still the fortune teller was not pleased and said he would make trouble if they married in Mintsing. When the couple learned that I would be in Nanchang, they came to join me at the hospital. After almost a year in Nanchang they were still certain they wanted to marry.

Because the New Life Movement had been working to reduce the customary expenses of Chinese weddings, mass weddings were provided. The couple decided they would be married in this new way, with a small religious ceremony afterwards. I felt honored when they asked me to stand in place of their parents. Beautiful Snow looked lovely in her yellow silk gown and rented veil. A car took her to the mass wedding hall, where I joined her. I found my way into the bride's room and found seven girls. Most of the other girls wore pink wedding dresses, with rather ugly artificial flowers on their heads and in their hands. A couple of the girls wore sloppy American dresses, with dirty sweaters underneath. Some brides were crying. One trembled violently. Another was in a terrible rage. Beautiful Snow, carrying a big armful of our best roses, stood serenely in the midst of this room full of chaotic emotions.

Then the brass band came marching in with a great blast, and the crowd pushed and rushed to see it. The ceremony had begun. The brides came single file out of their room, while the bridegrooms emerged to accompany their brides up the steps to the waiting officials. Able Strength was very handsome in his long blue Chinese gown and black jacket. Hwa Sing in pink, and Miss Liu's little girl in yellow, carried Beautiful Snow's bridal train. The ceremony was brief, photographs were taken, and the couples were then whisked away in taxis to their new homes. How different this wedding was from those I had witnessed in the years before in Mintsing. But that afternoon the religious ceremony was held in our parlor. Two tall red candles, traditionally a part of any Chinese wedding, stood on the preacher's table among dark red roses. The preacher married the couple again, and we sat down to a little feast which cost only thirty dollars. (The expense for the civil ceremony had been seven dollars.) Then the guests sat around eating watermelon seeds and talking pleasantly until ten at night. I had put fleurs-de-lis, red roses, and red candles in their room, with new window curtains and bedspread to match. The fleurs-de-lis symbolized deep love, while the roses stood for true love. And so the bridal day came to a close.

29
From Nanchang to Chungking

WHEN THE JAPANESE plunged China into a terrible war in the summer of 1937, I volunteered my services to the Chinese Red Cross. While awaiting notification from the Red Cross, I gathered the small group of friends who had accompanied me to Nanchang from Fukien. I told them I had volunteered for a dangerous service, and that I dared not keep Hwa Sing and Third-Sister-in-Law with me. I told them sadly that I was going to send both back home to Mintsing and asked them to decide themselves what they should do. As the Fukien group prepared to return home I sadly helped Hwa Sing pack her things. The next morning they departed. I watched the chair that bore Third-Sister-in-Law and Hwa Sing head down the mountain stairs of Kuling, where we had been vacationing. It seemed to me that I had lost almost everything that was precious to me.

Then I settled down to wait for information from the Red Cross. Rumors abounded. Then we began to receive news about the wounded. The bombing of Nanchang had left unburied dead everywhere. Some said that doctors were gathering at Wuku and Hankow to treat the many wounded, but no one could give details. I was still waiting to hear from the Red Cross and now began to wonder if my application had been received. Finally, late in September I responded to a telegram from Bishop Ralph A. Ward to go to Chungking. I packed my bags and walked down the mountain to Kiukiang to catch a boat up the Yangtze.

A British boat, loaded to the gunwales, arrived from the east. There was not even standing room. After a few hours another arrived, then another, but all were too full to take on even one more person. People were fleeing from the eastern seaboard on British boats, hoping that the Japanese would not bomb them. I concluded that if I expected to go further west I would have to take a Chinese boat, even with the chance of its being bombed.

Finally, late in the evening, two men who seemed to know me wandered in. "Doctor, where are you going, late in the evening and alone?"

"I am going to Chungking and I am thinking that perhaps I shall have to walk there."

"You do not remember us, but you treated our illnesses this summer on the mountain. We will help you get on the next boat."

By some miracle they shoved me aboard the next boat with a ticket in my hand. This boat, too, was packed solid. In the dining salon people had paid high prices for a stiff, straight-backed chair in which to spend the night and next day. I stood in the middle of the room, in the heat of tired bodies, standing hour after hour. Most of these people had come all the way from Shanghai, a journey of three days and nights. Gradually I learned the recent experiences of my shocked companions.

"The Japanese bombed a Red Cross train," someone said. "Hundreds of wounded soldiers were killed in this manner."

"They bombed refugee camps outside Shanghai," another told. "They killed many hundreds of women and children."

We reached Hankow the next afternoon, and I stayed there with some missionaries until I could get a ticket to Chungking. While I waited in Hankow I watched the city from behind sandbags as it was bombed viciously by the Japanese. In that attack 200 people were killed, and the hospital staff kept busy all night treating the wounded.

During my stay in Hankow I met many interesting people. Among them were Professor and Mrs. Kwei. He taught chemistry at Hankow University; she was one of six sisters, born in New York to a Chinese pastor who had married an American girl. I knew Mrs. Kwei's sister, Mrs. Chang Fu-liang, in Nanchang. Another sister had married James Y. C. Yen, whose books for illiterates were then selling by the million. Another sister was the wife of Amos Wong, a famous gynecologist in Peiping.

Many of the people I met in Hankow had just arrived from Peiping. "We students had to dress as coolies, amahs, farmers, or servants in order to pass through the Japanese lines," they said.

"The Japanese found a gold watch on the boy just ahead of me," said one young student, "and they shot him to death on the spot."

"One professor had a few books in his small piece of luggage; the guard said 'pass on,' but as he walked by the guard, the Japanese stabbed him in the back and killed him."

"The Japanese felt our hands as we passed them," reported another. "If our hands were calloused, we were allowed to pass by. If the hands were soft, the person was snatched out of the line and we saw him no more."

What shocking days these young men and women had experienced. Most of them had left families behind. They were traveling on to west China with very little money or clothing.

On September 29, 1937, I boarded a Chinese boat, the *Fook Yuen,* for Chungking. Chinese First Class entitled me to a windowless little cell with two hard bunks; a curtain served for the door. I brought bedding, wash basin, teapot, and six tiny tins of fruit for the trip. The cabin boy quickly filled the teapot with boiling water, and I settled in. A country girl of fifteen—who blew her nose with her fingers, hawked horribly, and spit all over—was my cabin mate. Outside the curtain young men lay on cots. The deck was packed solid with these little cots. Babies wailed all over deck, people here and there were gambling, and the conversation rose and fell in waves.

I learned that many of the young men on board were naval cadets. They showed great love for the forty-odd little ones who ran around between their cots. They talked and played with the children, held them in their laps and fed them bits of cake bought in Hankow. Chinese children generally did not receive any discipline until they were about seven years old; until reaching that age, traditionally regarded as the age of reason, they were given pretty much a free rein. One little child ran to me and asked, "What honorable country do you come from?"

I told her I was from the United States.

"Oh!" she exclaimed. "I thought you looked very much like a foreign person."

The naval cadets became very much interested in the two-volume work on Chinese art that I was reading, and they pored over the volumes hour after hour.

I finally found the way to the roof of the boat. From the roof I looked at the broad Yangtze, a coppery gold in the setting sun. White sailboats floated along on all sides. Lush foliage of green trees lined the banks. The pearl-gray sky, opal in places, was lined with gold. After two days in the stuffy cabin, I felt alive again out in the sunlight and wind.

After passing the city of Ichang, we entered the first of the famed Yangtze gorges. The hills became very high and closed in on the river from both sides. Enormous ledges loomed above us—immense rock cathedrals in red and blue, their irregular outlines sharply silhouetted against the gray sky. Pulpit-shaped masses of stone rose high above us, adorned with stalactites as large as tree trunks. In places enormous blocks of rock had broken away, leaving great cavities that resembled the windows of a gigantic cathedral. Strange towers, spires, pinnacles, and ramparts 2,000 feet high created the feeling of entering a vast sanctuary in dim, religious light.

Hacked out of the ancient rocks could be seen a rough narrow stairway, worn by centuries of trackers who through the ages had toiled and sweated in their harnesses to drag boats and heavy cargoes up the rushing river. The river, imprisoned between stone cliffs, roared wildly and boiled over tremendous boulders. Again and again, the current turned to rush back upstream, forming madly racing whirlpools up to 200 feet in diameter.

In places we could see tributaries far above come rushing over the top of a cliff and break into a waterfall, falling down the red-and-blue cliffs in soft, long threads of white silk. Sometimes these waterfalls did not reach the bed of the river, but fell through space until the water was transformed into delicate gray-blue mist that was carried down the gorge by the wind. Further down, the mist sometimes struck the face of a cliff, where it was transmuted into a waterfall with the suddenness of a rocket's flare. Occasionally we spotted an enormous cave up the face of a cliff, from which rushed a foaming green-and-white falls.

Sometimes, where the precipices rose to the heights in steps, we could see beds of luxuriant maidenhair ferns, azalea bushes, and feathery groves of bamboo. Here and there a small thatched-roof house would appear, nestled under a great overhanging cliff. Further up on grassy slopes were huts and villages. We could see white goats; and there were children skipping along on the terraced slopes. Great patches of Indian corn stretched up to the horizon, the red soil showing between green rows. After emerging from that first twenty-mile gorge we again found quietness and peace. The silvery gray water lay perfectly serene; gray-blue and gray-red cliffs and columns were painted on its clear surface, interrupted only now and then by the reflection of a white sail boat manned by two figures in blue.

We were being transported upriver by steam. But much of the freight was hauled up the Yangtze in great lumbering boats propelled by sails. When these boats approached a gorge they pulled into shore to a small village where they could hire trackers. The great sail was then hauled down. A huge rope made of braided bamboo fiber would be attached to a strong iron ring which circled the base of the mast. This rope, a quarter-mile or more in length, was then paid out to the trackers on shore, who attached their harnesses—strong white bands that went over one shoulder and under the other arm—to it. In single file the trackers then towed the freighter up through the rushing waters of a gorge. A man would stand in the prow to signal with his arms; another man provided a tempo for the trackers by beating a large drum. In the stern several men manned the bow-sweep to guide the boat in and out of whirlpools and around great boulders. Other men grasped long bamboo poles tipped with iron spikes, with which they pushed the boat away from the cliffs or boulders. Step by step in perfect unison, bent double with the effort of dragging the heavy vessel, the men slowly moved forward. And they sang hauntingly sweet melodies as they went.

We finally entered the western province of Szechwan. Throughout the great valley through which we were passing I saw brilliant patches of golden rape mingled with the green squares that were fields of cotton, rice, flax, and sugar cane. Rich green fields of tobacco reminded me of the Connecticut Valley, as did the fields of Indian corn that could be seen climbing up the hillsides. Fruits and vegetables filled in the rest of the space. From time to time we would see salt, coal, or iron mines. As we proceeded further west we saw great flocks of sheep.

At last, 400 miles from Ichang and through eighty-five stretches of rapids, the boat rounded a corner and there was Chungking. This ancient city was set on cliffs above the juncture of the Yangtze and Chialing Rivers. Its wall—white against a blue-gray fog—rose high on the cliffs, approached by a number of worn stone staircases which led upward through old gateways to the street levels. Above the wall we could see modern buildings: banks, department stores, hotels, and apartment buildings. The silvery Chialing River encircled the city from the right and met the muddy Yangtze which came down on the left. In the distance were the purple mountains of Szechwan.

The Yangtze appeared to be nearly a mile wide here, and boats of every description could be seen. River steamers and freighters pulled up on the south shore across from the city. Little launches and small boats plied back and forth across the strong current to carry passengers from one bank to the other. Here and there a sailboat rode smoothly over the water. I was told that the great Yangtze annually carried to the coast 40 million pounds of wood oil and 300 thousand tons of salt from this part of Szechwan. Its freighters came upriver laden in exchange with kerosene, silks, cotton yarn, and luxury goods—fancy soaps, powders, and perfumes. My boat eased in to the south shore as I stared at this city high in the air.

Miss Andersen, a beautiful girl of Swedish and Chinese descent, met me. It was so beautiful here that I felt I had entered a new world. Our little boat was rowed far upstream; then the swift current bore it rapidly down and across to the city's stone steps. We landed on a sandy shore beneath gray-blue cliffs. The beach was alive with traffic. Men and women were streaming up and down the stairs to and from the boats. Men were riding along the shore on tough little Mongolian ponies. Other men trotted under heavy burdens of salt, rice, wheat, vegetables, or fruit that they were bringing to the city. Many little booths had been set up for business right on the shore. Other men carried passengers in chairs. The scene was arrestingly beautiful and interesting—blue clothes against a raw sienna sand; the neutral browns and greens of bamboo-matted houses which stood on long poles against the blue-gray cliffs and stairs. Above all of this circled the white city wall, blue in the shadows.

We climbed the steep stairs to the city gate. The homes of the poor lined each side of the stairs. We went through the ancient gate, up more stairs, and on to the modern streets. In the hustle and bustle of traffic, clumsy old buses roared along seemingly unmindful of the pedestrians who somehow always leaped out of the way just in time. Rickshas careened around corners while men carrying sedan chairs padded swiftly along apparently undisturbed by the uproar around them. At the opposite end of this long street, we entered a little lane and arrived at the big mission house adjacent to the Syracuse-in-China Hospital. I had arrived at my new home.

Chungking

30

Obstetrics, Orphans, and General Feng Yü-hsiang

The Syracuse-in-China Hospital in Chungking had nearly 200 inpatients when I arrived. I was put in charge of obstetric, gynecological, and pediatric services. Immediately I had to do a Caesarean section. Then we operated on two women with enormous ovarian cysts. These were done under local anesthesia, and the patients came through so nicely that their friends came flocking to see me. In only a few weeks I took out a fifty-pound cyst, and then one that weighed fifty-five pounds. The last woman weighed only ninety pounds after the cyst's removal. More women with big abdomens came, since no one had died of the operation. I wondered how these poor women were able to keep their balance with such heavy tumors in them. Then I took out an eighty-pound cyst. This proved to be a complicated case, for there was very heavy bleeding from peritoneum, intestines, mesentery, stomach and uterus, which had all adhered to the tumor. The patient lost so much blood that she went into collapse. I poured a good deal of saline into her abdomen just before closing her up, and she survived. She left the hospital later weighing eighty-nine pounds.

The obstetrical clinic which I soon opened became very popular among the young educated wives who had fled to Chungking from the eastern cities. These women had more faith in Western medicine than did the more isolated people of Szechwan. Soon we had twenty-five to thirty beds filled in the maternity ward; later this number climbed to fifty-five and sixty. Two Chinese women doctors, recent graduates of Tsinan Medical School, now joined my work so we were able to handle increasingly large numbers of patients.

Our small pediatric service also began to grow, not so much as a result of our efforts, but more as a result of the war. Many war orphans had been shipped into Chungking by Madame Chiang Kai-shek. These children were gathered from devastated areas of China and shipped to orphan camps in Chungking. The children most in need of medical attention were sent to our pediatric wards. They ranged in age from three to ten; they were in severe shock as a result of the slaughter of their families, the burning of their homes, terrific bombings, complete desolation, starvation, thirst, and long travel under the worst conditions. Day after day these orphans would simply lay quietly in bed, not moving, not speaking, not feeding themselves. We fed them. We sat by their beds. We took toys to them and talked to them. We pulled them out of bed and rocked them. Little by little the stunned look would begin to leave their small faces and their eyes would brighten a little bit. Finally a child would sit up in bed and then feed himself. Soon after that he would begin talking. At that point, they would be transferred to the orphanage and their place would be taken by another child in shock.

In our work we sometimes were able to observe some of the fascinating Chinese modes of behavior that appeared so strange in the eyes of many Westerners who lacked experience in China. Sometimes these Chinese customs gave rise to real problems. A very poor woman, whose husband was at the front, gave birth to a baby boy. She wanted to sell the baby because she was too poor to support him. Nurse Thunder was married, but had never had a child. Her husband, who was in Hankow, had threatened to find a concubine if she did not produce a child soon. So Nurse Thunder dickered with the poor woman to buy the child. As soon as the transaction had been arranged she wired to her husband reporting the good news that she had just given birth to a baby boy.

Meanwhile, a very wealthy man and high official in the Nationalist regime brought in his wife to deliver her baby. His mother had ordered him to take a concubine if his wife did not produce a boy, so this was to be a most important delivery. For some reason the man had engaged a Chinese doctor, of whom we knew nothing, to do the delivery. He did a craniotomy* and the baby was born dead. The man was desperate and could not bear to tell his wife she had lost her baby. Nurse Pearl

* Performed when delivery proves impossible, this procedure breaks the fetal skull to reduce its size.

heard about this and told him about the beautiful baby boy that Nurse Thunder had already purchased. Through Nurse Pearl this man offered a sum greater than Nurse Thunder could afford. Thus the original bargain was broken, and he wired his mother that his wife had delivered a baby boy. Nurse Thunder was able to find another suitable child in a local orphanage, so in the end both couples were happy.

Two Russian women came to the hospital as my patients and I was much interested in their behavior. Since Chungking was now the capital of China, the Russian Embassy, and the fifty or sixty Russians connected with it, had moved to the city. I was greatly amused to discover that both of these women communists, though only mildly ill, expected the best and most expensive room in the hospital. They also had to have packs of cigarettes to support their chain smoking; special sheets had to be put on their beds. They had to have the ultimate in ease and comfort despite their philosophy.

We witnessed many heartbreaking situations in those days of war. A woman from Shanghai, only seven months pregnant, came in for delivery one day. I asked her what had happened. She explained that her husband was an officer in the army and had been ordered far into the southwest. She would not be able to travel so far under terrible conditions while pregnant. Nor did she want to stay behind, fearing they would be separated forever because of the unsettled conditions; so she had gone to someone to induce labor. When the baby girl was born the mother refused to look at it. When the father arrived, he too refused to see the baby. I realized why. They could not take the baby with them, so it was necessary to give it to someone. They would not allow themselves by looking at it to love it.

Our missionary, Nurse Alma, went shopping one day and noticed two young girls, fifteen and nine, sleeping in a sheep basket. "What are you doing sleeping in that basket?" she asked them.

"This is our home," the older girl told her. "Our family was killed by bombing so we kept walking and came here."

"How do you get your meals?" Alma asked.

The girl pointed to three stones on the ground by the sheep basket. An earthen pot was set on the stones. The girls used grass for fuel. In the pot the older girl boiled sweet potato skins. "I go to the mountain every day," she explained, "and cut enough wood to get a few pennies for food."

The nine year old showed signs of edema;* she was pale and said nothing at all. Alma brought her to the hospital. Many orphans wandered the streets at this time. Homeless, unloved, and hungry, they often slept on someone's doorsill while begging for food. Eighty such children had just been taken off the streets of Chungking and put in the new Orphan Home supported by the government. People said there were many hundreds of such children wandering through other cities in the province. Gradually more would drift into Chungking.

When my friend from Nanchang, Miss Liu Tai-ching, arrived in Chungking, she began doing social work for our hospital. She also became interested in one of the government orphanages. One day I accompanied her there on a visit. This was the orphanage established for the eighty poor, filthy boys and girls under ten who had been found on the streets of Chungking. I boiled eighty eggs to take as a present. When we arrived we were greeted by eighty bright faces that beamed with pleasure to receive visitors. They carried themselves straight, bowed politely, and then asked enthusiastically for a story. They were thrilled with the eggs and peanuts we brought them. A little love and care had already transformed their lives.

Even in Chungking we continued to meet a wide range of interesting people, foreign and Chinese. One night General Feng Yü-hsiang came to dinner at our house.† He was a tall man who must have weighed

* This malady is characterized by an excessive gathering of serous fluid in the tissues.

† Feng Yü-hsiang (1882–1948), popularly known as the "Christian General" and reputed to have baptized his troops with fire hoses, was one of the major warlords of North China before his power base was destroyed in 1930. Thereafter, though he occupied posts in the National government, he never again

200 or more pounds. He was big for a Chinese, but he carried himself well and appeared to be a man of high intelligence, though of few words. I had heard that early in life he had been caught by a rather fundamental sort of Christianity. I wondered if he had later been able to rework his religious values and longed to discuss the subject with him. One of the missionaries present asked General Feng if there was any message she could take from him to the United States when she went on furlough in the near future. "Tell them to help us kill the Japanese," he said.

General Feng then went on to say that he had met some missionaries in the North who were real Christians; they lived simply, used Chinese-style clothes and ate Chinese food. I had to choke back a laugh because the missionary who planned the dinner had served both cake and pie for dessert. Feng's criticism of missionaries who lived well in China was a frequent one offered by Chinese people of all classes; it was a problem that I too worried about during all my years in China. Feng had the reputation of supporting progressive programs that would build up China's strength. He hated waste and ostentation. It was said that after a certain high official in Nanking had built himself a palatial residence a few years before, General Feng, who was living in Nanking at the time, immediately put up a mud hut across the street on which he hung a sign. On this sign was written "Feng Palace."

31
Bombings and Pony Expeditions

THOUGH WE THOUGHT Chungking would make a difficult target for Japanese bombers, to be on the safe side the hospital was drilling a cave deep into the rock of Chungking. A constant rumbling and shaking

---

wielded real power. For a detailed biography of one of the most colorful Chinese leaders of the period, see James E. Sheridan, *Chinese Warlord: The Career of Feng Yü-hsiang* (Stanford, 1966).

deep down in the bowels of the earth beneath us could be heard all day long in the hospital. Blow by blow with hand chisels, the men had gone to a depth of thirty feet in the solid rock. They were now blasting a really capacious tunnel which would be able to house 200 patients if necessary. We felt very lucky that the city was situated on rock, a potential Gibraltar. We thought about Nanking, where there had been no rock to burrow into even had there been time to do so. Dr. Ch'en, chief surgeon at the Nanking General Hospital, who had now come to Chungking, told us that many people had been entirely paralyzed for days after the terrific shock of the bombing in December 1937. Yet, it really did not seem very likely that any bombing worth mentioning would come to the remote province of Szechwan. The mountains were so high, and so often the region was covered with clouds, that we thought it most unlikely that the Japanese would be able to cause much trouble here.

We were wrong. Heavy bombing began in February 1938. We had been free of bombs all winter because of the low-lying clouds which made it impossible for the Japanese to fly into the mountainous province. But when the cloud cover began to dissipate, air raid warnings began to blow. People ran in all directions as they headed for home or for cover. Some headed for the river, where boats waited to take them across to the opposite shore. Others dashed for the capacious city air raid shelter, a tunnel in the rock so enormous that the authorities intended to use it for a subway after the war. The bombings were costly to the Japanese too. Sometimes we were told that not one of the attacking planes had returned to its base. Some were shot down; others ran out of fuel and crashed in the mountains.

I had invited a friend for dinner on the evening of one of those first raids. The early warning screeched while I was on a call. The chair men poured sweat in their frenzied haste to get me within the hospital gates before the second blast, which meant the streets were to be cleared. The streets were jammed with rushing people—some empty-handed, some carrying valuables, some with children on their backs or dragging others by the hands. Rickshas tore by, sedan chairs careened this way and that. A great city was on the run. Everyone shouted as they went. When the second signal came, an unnatural silence fell over the city; the streets were empty and the city became as silent as a forest. It was eerie.

On this day I slipped quickly into our residence compound, running through the hospital grounds to get there, to find everyone waiting to sit down to dinner. My guest had been through bombings in Tientsin, Hankow, and Nanking and seemed quite undisturbed as we sat down to the table. We heard the deep throaty rumble of the planes high over us as they came nearer and nearer. Then my guest said, "They are almost directly over our heads. We should now go to the cave." Suddenly there was a tremendous explosion which shook the house and hurt our ears. Windows and doors swung in and out crazily. In the quiet that followed we heard the delicate tinkle of falling glass and watched the white powder of plaster sift slowly down in the air. I seized my guest and ran her into the hall. Then came one explosion after another to the accompaniment of rapid fire from the antiaircraft guns that were mounted on roof tops all around us.

When the raid was over we went out to the compound wall to look down on the Chialing River, its sandy shore hundreds of feet directly below us. We saw twenty-four black holes in the long stretch of sand. If the planes had been just a bit further south when they dropped their bombs, we and the hospital would have been blown to bits. We could see people lying all around on the ground below, still too dazed to get up.

Soon the wounded began to come in. Fractured skulls, broken legs and arms, bruises, cuts, shock, hemorrhages. More and more were carried through our gate. They had to be set down in the yard, where we tried to identify the serious cases as quickly as possible. Soon a call came for help across the river. I was one of the party that responded; we went to a village about a mile's walk beyond the Chialing River. One of the victims, a little girl, had had her arm blown off and had already died before we arrived. Many women lay moaning in great pain.

Bombing Victims in the Hospital Compound, Chungking

One, whose leg was broken, was nursing her small baby in spite of the pain. Another had had part of her face blown off. Another woman had already died, her arm and entire shoulder blown off, but her baby was still clasped tightly in her other arm and was hungrily tugging at her breast.

It was dusk when we arrived back at the hospital. The yard was packed with wounded on their litters. More and more came in on stretchers, in chairs, on people's backs, or walking by themselves. Two died in the yard before they could be helped. We operated all night long. For the next two or three days I felt nothing but shock at the indiscriminate massacre of innocent people. I could not really believe it had happened. My whole life in China had been geared to patching up bodies, and now an evil power high in the sky was recklessly and uncaringly hurling death at us. It did not seem real for quite a while.

Gradually I came to realize that I had to face up to the possibility of instant death. But as I saw more results of the bombing, death itself seemed something less terrible than the horrible crippling and living death that all too often occurred. It took time to live with that grim possibility. I was thankful that Hwa Sing was safe in Mintsing, while Hwa Hui was in comparative safety on the south side of the Yangtze. At last I accepted the fact that I was a mere atom in the scheme of things, and my only goal was to carry on from one day to the next.

Interestingly enough, the fundamentalist missionary who had assailed me so brutally on an earlier occasion because I did not believe in the Second Coming was not at all frightened by the bombings. She stood outdoors in the open during an attack, even near the wall where the blast might have hurled her over the precipice. "A bomb will not hit me unless God wants it to," she said cheerfully. I had to ask her why she thought her God wanted all of the hundreds of victims we saw in the city to be killed or injured. She did not feel it was necessary to answer my question.

One night I awakened to the sound of frightened voices and noise of nurses running back and forth. There was a fire by the river directly below the cliffs that supported our wall. We watched from the wall as the people below desperately tore off their thatched or bamboo-matted roofs. Firemen fought fiercely on the edge of the flames, but house after house was consumed as the conflagration crept up the steep slope. Trapped by the fire, families retreated further up against the hill until they came to the high city wall, which they could not scale. Quickly the hospital servants brought strong ropes and lowered them over the wall. One at a time women, children and men, each clasping a prized possession, were pulled up into our compound.

Soon the blaze billowed over the top of our wall. We manned the hoses, while the patients were rushed out of the hospital in good speed thanks to our air raid training. The flames rose even higher and sparks showered over us. The window panes were too hot to touch. Sparks came in under doors, and the wood began steaming. We lugged pail after pail of water to keep the hospital wet, and we saved the building. When the burn cases came in I used Horace's method; we cleaned each burn well and painted it with 5 percent tannic acid, which was followed by a painting of 10 percent silver nitrate to form a pliable crust.

The next morning I stopped by the wall on my way to work and looked down at the smouldering ruins. Families were already cleaning up the debris, digging out their mud stoves and fragments of tiles. By evening one man had put up a framework with enough tiles on it to cover a corner for sleeping. One woman had already set up a bed of old boards, with an umbrella hung over it. Others were putting the finishing touches on new frameworks covered with straw matting. By dark they were cooking rice in their mud stoves. A thousand families had been rendered homeless by the fire the night before, but one night later they were settled in again. With their bundles of salvaged clothing and bedding, and with their children gathered around them, they had overcome another obstacle and were ready to go on living. I remembered a similar scene years before in the county seat of Mintsing. Those families represented to me the spirit of China. Before the ashes were cold they had already begun to rebuild what had been destroyed.

On my afternoon off, once per week in the spring of 1938, I went riding with some friends. We crossed the Yangtze and rented ponies on the south bank. One day we rode up a mountain on long winding stone stairs to Old Scholar's Cave, a famous temple that sat high above the city and river. From this vantage point the city appeared as a leaf-shaped tongue of land between the Chinsha and Chialing Rivers, which united at the point of the leaf to form the Yangtze River.

We dismounted at the gate, as was considered polite, and walked up the stone steps into the temple courtyard. Wonderful old trees—beech, pine, and cedar—stood in the yard. A kindly monk came out to greet us. Mr. Tsai, our guide, introduced my riding companion, Katherine, saying that she was from America.

"Oh, she is American!" exclaimed the monk, surveying her with interest. Turning to me he said, "Then you must be English."

I smiled and asked, "Why does the Honorable Teacher think this humble one is from England?"

"Oh," he answered, "because you two do not look at all alike."

The monk led us through wide temple courtyards. On one side we saw men playing mahjong; women too were playing the game in dark little rooms on the opposite side. The monk led us up steep stone stairways as we moved from one court to the next. In each yard an altar sat opposite the entrance. Beside a cave were shrines to various gods. Incense burned before each. One was to the god of hunchbacks; an enormous number of burned-out incense sticks stood in front of him.

While we sat resting at the highest temple that was perched on the summit of the mountain, we talked to Mr. Tsai, our guide, about the religions of China. I was especially intrigued with the ancient Chinese theory of dualism, developed when our European ancestors were mere savages sleeping in caves and gnawing bones. This school believed that everything occurred in a balanced dualism, symbolized by *yin* and *yang* which were the fundamental principles of nature. Every person thus had his double in ghost form. I was reminded of Carl G. Jung's ideas. We returned to Chungking that day through fields of golden rape that made the mountain plateau gorgeous and fragrant. Then we went down hundreds of stone steps and crossed the wide Yangtze to the city in the gathering dusk. After such a day away from misery and the effects of war I felt deeply relieved and rested.

Indeed, these rides into the Chinese countryside and the world of nature held great appeal to others also; sometimes as many as seven or eight of us would ride together. One of our frequent companions was a Cantonese widower, an aeronautical engineer from M.I.T., who delighted us with his observations on Chinese art, history, politics, and other subjects. Once Mr. Tsai, who was secretary to a general, brought four military ponies for another trip. These were snorting, shining black beasts who tore along at a faster clip than any ponies we had ever ridden. Mr. Tsai assured us that they could travel all day long without rest and without any sign of fatigue. Our destination was to be Singing Happy Mountain, ten miles beyond Chungking University. The four coal-black stallions tore off like mad. While we were climbing steep stone stairs through a tightly packed village, one of the horses slipped and fell, smashing a few eggs in a basket set out for sale. With much yelling and gesticulating, a man seized the horse's bridle. I thought for a moment we were all going to be murdered, but Mr. Tsai settled it all very calmly by paying twenty cents for the damage.

It was a blistering day, and despite Mr. Tsai's faith in the ponies' durability, they began to pant. So we got off and walked till they were rested. As we approached the temple on the mountain, we met President Lin Sen coming down from the temple.* He was sitting in a simple, open country chair. He was plainly dressed and attended only by two men in plain clothes. There were no soldiers and no guns.

The temple we visited was beautiful. It sported a golden roof, deep red pillars, and decorations in soft gray-blue. It was unusually clean.

* An early activist in the anti-Manchu cause by the turn of the century, Lin Sen (1868–1943) became a prominent leader of the Nationalist party. He served as chairman of the National government, titular chief of state but with little power, from 1932 until his death.

Guests came here for quiet, and fresh clean rooms were available for those who wished to stay over night. A very pleasant woman and her husband were in charge and they gave careful attention to the comfort of each guest. In one of the guest rooms were displayed pictures of the "world's twelve greatest people." Six were Chinese, including Chiang Kai-shek, a female martyr to the revolutionary cause in the early twentieth century, and four men I did not know. The six foreigners were Pasteur, Romain Rolland, Magellan, Lenin, Voltaire, and Hindenburg. After eating bowls of noodles we gazed at the beautiful view below us, each one sitting quietly by himself. Indeed, we all seemed to attain peace within ourselves that day.

32
Refugees in Szechwan

IN JULY 1938, I accompanied some Chinese friends to Chengtu, the provincial capital of Szechwan. It was a lovely ride through fields of rice, corn, and kaoliang. There were few cars on the road; gasoline now cost $12 for five gallons. Buses were old and poorly maintained. We saw many men riding ponies. Wooden carts, piled high with merchandise, were each pulled and pushed by six sweating men. Though this was a heartbreaking form of transportation, it brought a living to thousands of men. We saw long lines of patient, plodding oxen loaded with hampers or sacks of rice and other staples. Some people rode in chairs or rickshas. A few men were walking, some with fans held to their foreheads to protect their eyes from the glaring sun.

The streets of Chengtu appeared to be much like the streets of other large Chinese cities that I had visited. They were mostly narrow and crooked. Often shops specializing in the same goods would gather on the same street. There was a street that sold keys and key chains. On another street one found only shoes made of black cloth. Another sold black skullcaps. Thus, by going to different streets one could find a vast array of articles—mops, wooden buckets, cheap jewelry, rattan furniture, earthenware, stove-length wood, black iron kettles, old iron and wire, piece goods, foreign-style clothing, coarse paper, writing paper, bath towels, hosiery, flashlights, soap, books, scrolls, ropes, candles, straw mats, fans, pens, knives and scissors, foreign drugs, Chinese drugs, embroideries, wines, wooden flutes, brass trumpets, leather shoes and belts, straw sandals, full-length sheepskin coats, firecrackers, reed baskets, reclining chairs, huge straw hats, new and used rickshas, perfumes and powders. Indeed, the variety seemed endless. In addition, butcher shops, grocery stores and eating places—where well-browned chickens hung by their heads in rows—were plentiful.

In Chengtu I met many Chinese intellectuals, intensely patriotic, who had fled the Japanese terror in the east. Some were from Peiping, others from Tientsin; a large number had come from the major cities of the Yangtze. They told stories of horrible bombings. They had been witnesses to wholesale looting, burning, butchery, and raping by the Japanese invaders. This had made them firm in their commitment to fight to the end.

I came back to Chungking via Mt. Omei* (where I met my old friends Olin and Esther Stockwell from Mintsing) to find the city jammed with refugees. Every boat that came upriver now was packed with more shocked and exhausted people. Many also carried ammunition. The boats then returned downriver filled with soldiers. Some people believed that Chungking would be the last stand in China's resistance; but others had great faith in the prediction of H. G. Wells, who had said years before that Japan would attack China but would get no further inland than Hankow. His book, in both English and Chinese versions, was tremendously popular in Chungking in those days, but I found that the better-informed Chinese I met were not so optimistic.

By November 1938, the province had received so many refugees that the village wells outside Chungking could supply no more. All of

* Mt. Omei is one of the Four Sacred Mountains of Chinese Buddhism.

the temples were filled with people. Kerosene could no longer be purchased, and even candles were hard to buy. Transportation was difficult at best. Thousands of young students continued to arrive; many had walked for more than six months to reach Chungking from the coastal cities. They were housed in the temples under the most Spartan conditions. There was little food and no facilities for bathing.

By the end of 1938 more than 80 million people had arrived in Szechwan. Roughly 10 million of these were absolutely destitute. Mothers with their children had walked for over two months from Hankow; many died on the way, while others arrived in the province as orphans. Now when the government made an effort to gather all of the orphan-beggars in Chungking, instead of 80 there were 400 and more. Five thousand unclaimed children occupied one camp. They were barefoot in the bitter cold. Occasionally parents would appear to claim a child, but more often the children had to be shifted to orphanages.

As the refugees arrived, they were assigned to camps and given ten cents each to purchase their meals in street shops. An effort was made to find employment for them; gradually cooperatives were set up. Large areas of land were turned over to penniless refugees, while cattle, tools, and seeds were advanced to them. The government also established a Refugee Training Factory, where towels, stockings, mats, toys, shoes, and a number of other much-needed articles were produced. Though the social and economic problems were by no means solved, I was impressed by the government's attempts to deal with the refugee situation at a time when every effort was being made to resist the Japanese invasion. Compared to the bleak social services record of the warlord era, the results of which I had seen personally, the central government's work now seemed to indicate the beginning of a new era. For many of us foreigners who had lived many years in China, this record of achievement in face of terrible adversity could only be lauded. We were not unaware, naturally, of the numerous inadequacies of the program. Squeeze and corruption were still part of the Chinese scene, but there were also thousands of honest, hard-working people who were dedicated to the improvement and strengthening of their nation. These people were producing significant results.

As I watched people pouring off the boats—as many as a thousand a day—only to be pushed further west for lack of room, I wondered why the United States smugly continued to sell ammunition to Japan. What sort of people and what kind of foreign policy would allow such a thing? My own country, which, in terms of history, had only a short time before fought so nobly for its independence, now appeared to be aiding an aggressor against a nation that was fighting for its independence. I was sickened.

While thousands poured into Chungking every week, and thousands more pushed on further west, business in the city thrived. New restaurants, built by refugees from Peiping, Canton, Amoy, and other coastal cities, were packed with refugee customers happy to get their own provincial cuisine. Cafes that supplied butter and coffee appeared, mute evidence of the arrival of a large number of wealthy refugees who were accustomed to foreign foods. Six new theaters, which showed Chinese, Russian, and American films, were filled nightly. The Russian films were excellent and had great appeal, while the American ones were trashy.

Colleges sprang up like mushrooms in western China as students and faculty fled the Japanese. The National Maritime College trained steamship officers; the National Technical Institute turned out skilled tradesmen; the Kun Vocational School taught iron work. The China Vocational School gave courses in architecture, mechanics, and engineering. The National Central Industrial College taught chemistry, electrical engineering, and carpentry. The Woman's Vocational School taught spinning, weaving, and some agricultural subjects. I was told that altogether forty-seven industrial schools and thirty-six agricultural schools were being opened in China's West.

Because roads for trucks to bring freight in over the high mountains from the South were so inadequate, the government bought 1,000 carts, each to be manned by six men. A team of this kind could make the trip in forty days with a loaded cart. Our mail came by mule train over that long trail. Though Japan had so intimidated France that she no longer dared to openly ship munitions into China from Indochina, nevertheless countless cases labeled "Baby Carriages" did arrive on the carts.

When we heard that Hankow had fallen, even though we had expected it, it was a deep blow to everyone. We heard that Madame Chiang Kai-shek had personally directed the city's evacuation. Many of the women had been sent out already and many had arrived in Chungking. Poor people had been sent to villages outside of Hankow. When all the preparations had been made, Madame Chiang left on her plane. Then her soldiers systematically bombed all the bridges, the airport, railway stations, government buildings, and all public utilities. Then they, too, retreated into the mountains in the west from where they planned to carry on guerrilla warfare against the Japanese.

When the Japanese took possession of Hankow they bombed boats of refugees. Many were sunk and thousands lost their lives. We also heard that a train packed with women and children refugees had been bombed; the passengers had been machine-gunned when they ran from the burning coaches.

I was shown photographs taken from the bodies of dead Japanese soldiers in Nanking. Some showed Chinese soldiers, drenched with oil, on fire; others showed soldiers and farmers being burned alive. Others gave grim evidence of the slaughter of little children. Many girls had been stripped of their clothing and photographed. One picture showed a young woman who had had two long sticks pushed into her vagina and had been left to die. When we heard Canton had also fallen to the Japanese, there was further weeping and heartache in Chungking.

When Madame Chiang arrived in Chungking, a New Life Movement banquet for 400 guests was given in her honor. This was on January 3, 1939. Madame Chiang delivered an impassioned speech; her spirit was infectious. I found her to be a rather small but handsome woman; she was charming, but at the same time displayed the talents of an organizer and executive. Unfortunately, she spoke the Shanghai dialect, which I found difficult to understand. She was accompanied by her old Australian friend, William H. Donald, who was now her trusted adviser. He had accompanied her on her trip to return the Generalissimo from captivity in Sian on Christmas Day, 1936. He was an elderly, genial man. It was apparent that he was very loyal to her.

33
Work in Tzechow

CHUNGKING WAS GIVING me a great deal of experience in obstetrics and gynecology. I and the two young Chinese women doctors looked after about sixty patients in these categories who were in the hospital at a given time. By the summer of 1939 I felt much better equipped to return to Mintsing to continue my work there. But it was still impossible to get back to Mintsing because of the Japanese. Because our Chungking hospital was planning to break up into small sections and move into the country to escape the bombing, and because I still could not return to Fukien, I accepted an invitation to move to the hospital in Tzechow. Tzechow was roughly halfway between Chungking and Chengtu.

The hospital lent me the car. Two refugee nurses, who volunteered to go with me, traveled with me all day on the road toward Chengtu through gorgeous fields of rape and through beautiful mountain scenery. We arrived in Tzechow just at dusk, crossed the river on a small ferry, and found our lodgings at the hospital.

As soon as the hospital work was organized properly, I threw a party for the Board of Managers and for all of the important city officials. Thirty men arrived with the mayor, a rather young and rotund man who was followed by a servant. After a good meal I made the necessary speech. I told the group I hoped we could together plan programs which would benefit the community, and mentioned health education, village clinics, and a few other possibilities.

Then we conducted the group through the hospital. They saw a man recovering from an appendectomy. Another man had had a bullet removed from his stomach. We had just amputated the arm of another man. They saw a young woman who had cut her throat and trachea, but who was now well on the way to recovery. Yet another man had come thirty miles in a chair, dripping blood from a bullet wound all the way. Just above his elbow we had found an ugly piece of iron, such as bandits use, and removed it. A boy was being treated after being struck by lightning. We had several interesting cases to show them, and they were quite impressed.

Later the mayor invited me to a meeting on disease prevention at his headquarters. I went with the Chinese woman doctor who had joined me from Chengtu. We found the mayor had also invited ten ignorant practitioners of Chinese-style medicine. We were all asked to speak in turn concerning the cholera epidemic that threatened the city. I spoke last and suggested that we put short articles in the local newspaper telling people something about cholera and its prevention. I also suggested distributing small pamphlets giving such information, as well as public lectures. I offered also to give free inoculations.

But it was all too evident that only I and my companion really wanted to educate the public. The others did not want Western medicines to be used, even to treat cholera. Yet, in the mayor's office were posted several mottos written in large gilt characters: When you see a good deed to do, you must be as brave as the men of old; Officials must consider every duty important; Help people to attain happiness; Education, for all the world. I could not help being struck by the contrast between such admirable ideals and the actual thinking and behavior of the man who used them to decorate his office.

The cholera hit suddenly and viciously in July. The mayor's son was one of the first victims. By the time he called me, after the boy had been treated unsuccessfully by the native practitioners, the boy was unconscious. We gave him saline intravenously and he rallied. His father was so pleased that he sent him to our hospital for further treatment. Three more children came in that day with the same disease; all four lived.

The next day we had two wards full of cholera patients. We kept very busy giving them saline. On arrival these men and women were often unconscious, their feet and hands wrinkled from water loss. If conscious, they were very restless and suffered terrible cramps. Their eyes were deeply sunk. Our small staff was inadequate to cope with such an emergency, so we hired young schoolgirls to help. We also hired a woman to make more sheets, a smith to make bedpans, and a carpenter to make more beds.

A few of the patients died, so I began to digitalize* each one as he was admitted. At the same time we launched a campaign of inoculation; in the first week we gave 1,500. The death rate of cases treated by the old-style Chinese practitioners was very high, but we had no exact statistics. One of the very few that died under our care was the wife of a local teacher. She left six small children; at her funeral friends and neighbors wept as they looked at that row of poor little children. The five-month-old baby was starving for lack of milk, so I took him into my house to nurse him to health. I called him David. In time the epidemic subsided and finally died out altogether.

In August, one of the three missionary women at the hospital became ill. I thought a few weeks of rest in cool hills might be good for both of us, so we headed for the nearest resort. We rode in terrible heat through thirty kilometers of country laid out in squares and rectangles of varied colors. The ripening corn showed golden against patches of green beans, cotton or peanuts. The sugar cane patches were fresh light green, while the kaoliang produced brown squares because of its rich brown tassels. The wheat fields appeared in deep green. We passed fields of cotton and could see rice paddies, in dark green shapes, that

* To treat with digitalis, a cardiac stimulant.

lay lower in the valley. As we traveled over gently rolling hills on the narrow, winding paths that held to their crests, we passed houses from time to time. Some had tile roofs, but more commonly they were thatched. White geese and ducks, along with dirty-faced children, were in evidence all along the way. Now and then we met a dwarf, for they were not uncommon in that area. We passed men loaded with salt or oil who jogged along the trails beneath their burdens. We saw caravans of stallions, mules, or heifers in long trains carrying salt or coal. I was told that the mares were kept on the western plains for breeding. That night we stopped at High Stone Market and stayed in a very dirty inn. Our room was right over the pig pen and its smell. The pig pen was the only toilet facility. As in all other inns along the way, relieving oneself involved perching on the pig fence.

The next morning we left at 4:00 A.M., hoping to cover another thirty kilometers. Three of our bearers became sick along the way, however, so I got some hot water in a village and prepared soda for them. Instantly, it seemed, everyone in the village produced a cup and asked for a dose of soda. Because it was white they apparently thought it was "cold" medicine, very fitting for such a hot day. That night we stopped at another dirty inn with armies of bedbugs. On the third day we reached High Stone Steps, a wonderfully cool resort with fresh pine fragrance in the air. This place was frequently visited by vacationing missionaries. We found about thirty-five foreigners there, half of them children. They had all come from a radius of less than 100 miles. We enjoyed the conversation with these people, the smell of pine, and the magnificent view. It was hard to imagine a war was going on not far away.

When we returned to Tzechow, thoroughly rested, I amused myself by learning the couplets that were sung out by the chair men. The first line was a warning from the first man of what lay ahead; the second line was the acknowledgment of the man in the rear. "Great strength" referred to a cow or horse, while "man on the ground" indicated the presence of any person near enough to be bumped by the chair.

"Ahead an obstacle doth appear; we give way here in the rear."
"Great strength stands ahead; steer clear and nothing said."
"Umbrella on the right there; tear it to pieces, I don't care."
"Wet and slippery I say; like a wave of water on the way."
"I see clouds in the sky; a man on the ground I spy."
"Nice round little heap; I shall guard my step."

I settled down to work again in Tzechow. When I had taken in the five-month-old David, he was unable to raise his head or move his hands. I bought four milk goats and he began to thrive immediately on their milk. The word spread quickly and other people began to send their sick babies to me. One well-dressed couple brought their baby all the way from Chengtu, reporting that the doctor there said he could do nothing for the baby. The baby shrieked in pain and was drenched in perspiration; his fists contracted over his thumbs and his legs contracted on his thighs. "I can cure him," I told the parents. I gave him goat milk and extra calcium. In three days he was well.

More babies came so I bought more goats. But then the goats, one at a time began to die. Eventually I learned that they were dying of a parasite that came from infected grass. So I shifted to soybean milk which we made ourselves. The babies did so well on this formula that people made special expeditions to see the "foreign babies," which they called them because they were being nurtured by a foreign method.

One day in the fall of 1939 a man brought his twelve-year-old son to us. It was a pitiful case. The boy had a tumor hanging out of his mouth. The father reported that when he was three a small swelling appeared below his right eye. I found that the growth had begun in his maxillary sinus. As it grew, it moved downward and broke through the roof of the boy's mouth, pushing out the upper gum. It grew right out through the mouth. His mouth was, in fact, no longer visible. When he ate he had to push the food up under the mass of tumor. His hemoglobin count was only 40; his red count was only 2,000,000. I did not think the growth was malignant since it had been present for nine years.

After clearing up a bad case of hookworm, I cut a small hole in the boy's neck and inserted a tube. When he had become accustomed to breathing through the tube, we operated on the tumor, administering ether directly through the tube. It was necessary to go up through the mouth to reach the root of the tumor. But the years of growth had left the boy badly disfigured. His upper jaw had been badly pushed out of shape in front, while the lower jaw projected far forward; his nose had grown over to the left side, and his mouth had been torn at the corners by the growing mass. We removed the tumor and repaired the corners of his mouth. The nose, jaws, and cheekbone we had to leave to nature. I had taken photographs of him before we operated. In six months we would see what nature had done for him.

The next morning, very pleased with myself, I went to see the boy. He was crying. I asked someone what had happened and was told that he had never been allowed to see himself in a mirror. Now someone in the ward had given him one, and when he saw what he looked like, he began crying.

"What is the worst thing you saw in that mirror?" I asked the boy.

"That big bump on my cheek is very ugly," he sobbed.

It was true. The tumor had pressed the right maxillary sinus way out on the cheek. I thought for awhile and finally told him I would remove the bump if he was willing to have another operation. The boy was very pleased. A few weeks later we scraped out the whole area, leaving just the periosteum.* The operation was a great success. Six months later he returned. He had grown so much I hardly recognized him. His mother and father were overflowing with joy, and the boy's face was indeed very presentable even though the right eye socket was higher than the left. Again we took photographs, and I planned to write the case up for the *China Medical Journal*.

By November 1939, we had managed to stock our public reading room with paperbacks in Chinese. It was open to anyone who wished to

* Periosteum is the fibrous membrane that covers bones.

come. I also took books to the wards and private rooms every day. In a ward someone would read aloud to the others, which usually resulted in much discussion of what the book had to say. We offered books on religion, philosophy, medicine, agriculture, sociology, and other subjects. From time to time I checked all the books over to see which were the most worn in order to get some idea of their preferences. Leslie Dixon Weatherhead's *The Mastery of Sex* was the most soiled and worn volume in the collection, but *Romance of Medicine, Little Girl Lost,* Samuel Moor Shoemaker's *Twice Born Ministers,* and a copy of *The Life of D. L. Moody* were also well used.

In January 1940, a group was sent to Tzechow from Chungking with an ambulance full of gauze and drugs to be distributed to expected bombing targets. Our hospital looked forward to receiving these supplies, but to our dismay, the mayor had established a small pseudo-hospital at the gate of the city. When any group was sent by Madame Chiang, the New Life Movement, or other organization to Tzechow, the mayor immediately steered them to his small hospital. The mayor always managed to keep such parties from visiting our hospital. But this time the party from Chungking was led by the clever Mr. Liu. Our staff discussed the problem and decided that this time they would go over to the mayor's hospital and show themselves. As a foreigner I thought it best to stay out of sight. But seven of our nursing graduates, dressed in crisp white uniforms and well-starched caps, marched down the road with Dr. Jiang, our druggist, Mr. Li, the laboratory man, Chĭeng, and his assistant, Mr. Ko. I was very proud of them as they walked toward the city gate and thought that Mr. Liu would have little trouble recognizing our personnel as the city's best hospital staff.

Our group carried ordinary-looking boxes which held emergency supplies for immediate use after a bombing. The other group had equipped its personnel with fine-looking boxes, but they were known by Dr. Jiang to be empty. When it came her turn to meet Mr. Liu she said, "What nice little boxes this hospital has given its staff. How wonderful it would be if we had such boxes."

Mr. Liu caught on right away and he asked to see the handsome boxes. When he opened one it was empty. Then he asked to see the very common boxes of our group and found that they had been carefully and fully stocked. When Mr. Liu quizzed the two groups on procedures for treating bombing victims, our well-trained group performed beautifully; the mayor's employees did not even know how to properly bind wounds. So our staff returned with the good news that our hospital had been awarded the drugs and gauze. But the mayor had lost much face, and I feared we would pay in the end for the present good fortune.

34

My Last Days in China

THE SUMMER OF 1940 in Szechwan was unusually hot. Dr. Jiang, my Chinese partner at the hospital, came down with tuberculosis, leaving all of the hospital's responsibilities in my hands. Hwa Hui, the older of my adopted daughters, had graduated as a nurse from the Canadian Hospital in Chungking, so it was arranged that she would come to help in Tzechow. But with the heavy work and the shortage of food I became so weak that I finally could not climb stairs without sitting down to rest on the way. I had lost a lot of weight, and everyone was alarmed. By the fall they insisted that I go on to Chengtu for medical care.

Hwa Hui and I tried to get on a bus, but every one was packed with refugees moving westward. Finally we engaged chairs to take us the 140 kilometers to Chengtu. Off we went wrapped in blankets, carried by strong fast men. We traveled over the Great Western Road, a stone-paved, three-foot-wide path that ran from the eastern seacoast to the far boundaries of China to the west in Tibet. The path had been used for centuries; every stone was well worn.

We saw families out digging sweet potatoes and peanuts and gathering the potato vines for fodder to feed their goats during the coming winter. Cleared fields were being prepared to plant winter wheat and beans. Women sat in the fields on low stools wielding axe-like implements with two long prongs, with which the ground was readied for planting. The waxberry trees, with their red foliage and snow white berries, showed against the soft blue of distant mountains. Cedars stood by the way, and great fields of sugar cane rustled in the breeze. In places the path was bounded by tall grasses twenty feet high; their gray-white plumes shown silver in the setting sun.

This ancient highway was busy. Men bent beneath loads of sweet potatoes, peanuts, rice, or sugar which they carried in twin baskets attached to their shoulder sticks. Women traveled with babies strapped to their backs. Old women and children carried baskets of fresh-cut grass for fuel or for the family buffalo. Other children led the family pigs or buffaloes out to graze. It seemed that everyone was chewing on a stick of sugar cane two to three feet long. We passed through little villages, with small houses set close to the path on either side. Village restaurants, their stoves perched on the edge of the highway, catered to villagers and travelers alike. The fuel for these stoves appeared to be corn cobs. We stopped to eat. Next to the stove was a row of white enamel wash basins, which were filled with raw, leafy vegetables. From a pole hung meats of different cuts. A great wooden steamer of cooked rice sat ready. We sat at a bare wooden table on sawhorses. A dirty waiter brought bowls to us after wiping them out with the corner of his equally-dirty apron. Then he brought us bowls of boiling water. Meanwhile the cook was making a cabbage soup, delicious after a long day of riding.

The second day of the trip followed a motor road, so we hired rickshas. My ricksha boy turned out to be a grateful patient whom I had treated in Tzechow. He pulled his heart out, up hard hills, through thick yellow mud and down long hills where he had to run for his life to keep ahead of the vehicle. The rickshas were old and bare, the springs tied up with strings, ropes, and cowhide thongs.

On this road the country's produce went to market on wheels. The most common vehicle was a little wheelbarrow that was set very low. The farmers transported loads of sugar cane on these small vehicles. In addition, we saw two-wheeled carts with rubber tires. These were drawn by a man in the shafts, helped by others who pulled ropes on each side. Three or more men brought up the rear, pushing uphill and holding the cart back downhill. These carts were loaded with cotton, iron, wire, cloth or thread.

In Chengtu an enterprising dental surgeon pulled my five best front upper teeth. He thought that some infection in them had caused my poor health. I hoped he was right. But as the weeks progressed it became evident that the teeth had not been the problem. The bishop ordered me to go on furlough. While I waited I visited several cooperatives in Chengtu. In one women carded wool, spun yarn, and made cloth and sleeveless sweaters. The wool had been dyed a beautiful red-brown with banyan tree bark. One of the Y.W.C.A. cooperatives sheltered sixty girls who were learning tailoring, weaving, and mass education. I was more than thrilled to see, in 1940, the kind of projects developing that I had felt were so necessary when I had arrived in China in 1924. Now my hopes and dreams seemed to be coming true.

Finally I had to leave. A high-ranking military official called to say goodbye. To my astonishment he turned out to be the officer who had given me the pony to use in Mintsing my last year there. Another high-ranking officer sent me an expensive merit board in black lacquer with letters of pure gold. Though it was a great honor, I would have preferred that the money had gone to buy rice for hungry patients. A crowd followed me through the city street to the river's edge, and many of them crossed to see me off. Luckily I found a ride on a truck that was going all the way to Chungking.

When I boarded the airplane in Chungking I found my old friend Olin taking the same flight. We waited for hours to take off. When we arrived that evening in Hong Kong, we learned that the plane that had taken off just before ours had been shot down; everyone on it had been killed.

Before we left Hong Kong, the British inspectors went through my scant baggage and found my pile of scrapbooks, which over the years I had filled with clippings from Chinese newspapers. One book was filled with reports on agricultural projects, and there were others on industry, cooperatives, reconstruction, refugees, transportation, war orphans, medicine and education. The inspector informed me I had to take them to the censor's office before leaving. I was afraid what the censor would do to my collection, so I took only two. With great shears the august censor solemnly cut out the newspaper clippings and mutilated the books. He saw nothing wrong in my taking the clippings once they had been torn from the books. So I made a false bottom to my suitcase and put in the unmutilated scrapbooks. I felt very lawless, but could see no reason why my years of labor on those books should be brought to nothing. As I boarded the ship to Shanghai my blouse bulged with the letters and newspaper items the censor had cut from the books. No one searched my suitcase when we boarded, nor did they when we entered Japanese-held Shanghai.

I arrived in Shanghai in an ancient battered hat, a borrowed coat, shoes that were too big for me, queer old riding gloves, and hair that had never known a permanent. I had now entered a world of smartly dressed, more-or-less sophisticated city people.

"I feel rather passé," I said to the missionaries who met me.

"Never mind. Folks just think you're a Russian refugee," they said.

I knew then that I should polish up before taking the ship to the United States. I went to buy a hat. The sales lady handed me a queer-looking straw object, in navy blue, with an elastic band to go behind the ears. She assured me it was a hat.

My missionary companion said, "You know it must be a hat because you are buying it in a hat store."

I put it on and looked in the mirror. "I look like a clown," I said.

"Really it is very becoming," they assured me.

"How much is it?" I asked the sales lady.

"Forty-nine dollars and fifty cents," she said.

Then I knew it must be a hat, even though in those days $49.50

in Shanghai was only $2.75 in gold. I walked off leaving the old battered hat on the aristocratic counter.

"You should have brought it along," chided my companion. "Some refugee might be glad to have it."

"Even refugees have their self-respect," I said. Then I got a permanent and some new clothes so that I could be admitted to the United States when I arrived.

When I arrived in Northampton, Massachusetts late in the evening, no one had come to meet me. My mother had had a cerebral accident some time previously, and she had not remembered my telegram. I soon realized I could not return to the China I loved, for I was the only child who could now care for her. She had given her whole life to her five children and had worked hard and sacrificed much to see that we had an education. She had been ever alert to instill in us high ideals for the future. Now it was my turn to care for her in her failing years, for her weary mind had gone to rest before her strong New England physique had worn out.

Since the doctor in our small town, Williamsburg, had gone into the army, people were clamoring for medical help. I bought a car and began driving through the beautiful Berkshires making home calls, in strange contrast to the rounds I had made in the hills of Mintsing. I attended people now at the Northampton Hospital and held office calls in my home. It was a novel and exciting experience to practice medicine in my own tongue, among my own people, in the town where I grew up.

Postscript

MY LIFE as a medical doctor and educator in village and urban China that spanned eighteen unforgettable years, from 1924 to 1941, thus came to an abrupt end. On my return home to New England, I was thrust suddenly back into the Western world. I experienced a great shock; incredibly, not until then had I really been aware of the great differences between the peoples of China and America.

The Chinese I had viewed for so many years, whatever their particular foibles, had learned great patience from centuries of suffering, philosophy and discipline from Confucianism, and calmness from Buddhism. They were a capable, proud, industrious, intelligent, and intuitive people who possessed keen powers of observation. They were dignified, cheerful, and had fine senses of humor. There was a great love of nature among the people I knew in China, whether they were boatmen or scholar-officials. They lived close to nature and knew her moods. The sky was their father and the earth their mother. They loved the mountains, lakes and streams, the trees and flowers. They knew the properties of their herbs and wild plants, which were freely used in their medicines. They were invariably polite, and carefully observed the amenities required in various relationships. In addressing people, the gentleman or the laborer would use great humility, mentioning their poor and miserable sons, their wretched homes, their lack of decent food for a guest. The Chinese were careful in speech, wishing to keep guests easy and comfortable and, at all costs, to save face. These were customary courtesies that put people at ease.

The Chinese loved big families. They loved to be in a crowd. They were happy with children running all over the house, with family and neighbors reading their letters, learning their secrets. I think it was hard for them to understand foreigners with their privacy and locks, their sleeping in single rooms, or their enjoyment of an evening or a walk alone. But they were always courteous and permissive toward us.

When I arrived in the United States in May 1941, I sensed with shock some of the differences between the two civilizations. Perhaps it was the lack of self-discipline that first struck me: children guzzling soft drinks, gobbling ice cream, sucking on candy at all hours. Their parents smoked and drank freely, blurring out their mental faculties with over-indulgence. There was a great demand for comfort on every side. No one would put up with an hour of insomnia or headache, but went to a doctor to relieve his little discomfort. People were preoccupied with sex.

Having returned from a China which suffered so much, I was struck by my memories of these people who were now struggling against tremendous odds to secure a better life. In this historic struggle China was bursting with revolution against the evil bonds which had held her down. On the other side was my own country which lived in complacency and self-indulgence. People seemed unaware and indifferent to the plight of other countries in Asia which were so much less fortunate. Americans seemed to be stained with the sense of superiority, insensitive to the urgency for a real peace on earth.

Even now in 1974, with my mind still shuttling back and forth between these two great nations which are based on different civilizations, I feel frustrated and unable to share my thoughts; I yearn to withdraw from this philosophy of ease and comfort. But most of all I wonder about the future of the United States and China.

Yet even as a person must experience hardship, suffering, and bereavement to attain maturity, it may be that our own country, like China already, must be bathed in tears and blood in order to find itself in its rightful place of simple equality among the nations of the world. For it is through pain and heartbreak that humility is born; and it is from humility that wisdom and understanding come. Physical deprivation, hardship, bereavement—these may not be evils but blessings if they initiate constructive change.

Indeed, China and the United States possess their individual strengths and weaknesses. One mistake of too many Western missionaries to China was the conviction that they bore to the East all the good tidings and all the knowledge of a better way of life. Now many of us realize that abilities and defects are equally shared in the midst of our diversities. What is desperately needed between our two nations are bridges of good will. But these must be two-way bridges, with traffic flowing both ways. There will not be a return of missionaries over that bridge, but businessmen, newspapermen, technical workers, tourists, and perhaps doctors and nurses may venture across it. Many of us who lived in China long years ago learned something from its ancient civilization and the courage of its people; perhaps China too has found something worthwhile from our relatively raw mode of life.

As I look back on my life in Mintsing and Central China, I reflect that we did our basic medical and educational work with a maximum of the strength of our hearts and minds and bodies, but with a minimum of cash. Many missionary and government-sponsored projects, which were put on with a fanfare of donations and a staff including many college-trained personnel, failed. But I felt our little, unassuming effort to educate villagers was successful *because* of its small size and its lack of any ostentation or funds. The point was to communicate new ideas in a manner that could be understood by the common people; to accomplish this, money was not the essential factor. Obvious to some of us at the time, but too little recognized by the Kuomintang government, this basic receptivity at the village level for information that would improve conditions provided an unquenchable source of power. This fact was not ignored by China's communist leaders who showed concern for China's suffering poor. The present regime is now carrying on with personnel who are educated in the basics and who approach the villagers with modesty. Like our staff forty-odd years ago, these modern barefoot doctors work in the fields when free from medical responsibilities.

Though my story is the view of an American medical missionary, it is my earnest hope that it accurately reflects to Western readers something of the quality of life in China during the painful decades before the Communist revolution.

RUTH V. HEMENWAY
Williamsburg, Massachusetts
February 1974

Editor's Note

ON FEBRUARY 10, 1974, Dr. Hemenway celebrated her eightieth birthday with a large gathering of family and friends in Northampton, Massachusetts. Among the well-wishers was her first adopted daughter; in 1955 Rachel Chin (Little Thunder, Hwa Hui) had come with her husband, Neng-wong, and children, Sara and John, to live with Dr. Hemenway in Williamsburg.

Two months later Dr. Hemenway suffered a series of strokes that ended her more than half-century-long medical career. She died July 9, 1974, having completed a life of devoted service to both Chinese and Americans. Many will remember her indomitable spirit that brought new courage to those she served.

Library of Congress Cataloging in Publication Data
Hemenway, Ruth V. 1894–1974.
Ruth V. Hemenway, M.D.: a memoir of Revolutionary China, 1924–1941.
1. Hemenway, Ruth V., 1894–1974. 2. Missionaries, Medical—China—Biography. 3. China—Description and travel—1901–1948.
R722.32.H45A37 1977 951.04′2′0924 [B] 76-45245
ISBN 0-87023-230-4